Integrated Marketing Co........

The Marketing Series is one of the most comprehensive collections of books in marketing and sales available from the UK today.

Published by Butterworth-Heinemann on behalf of The Chartered Institute of Marketing, the series is divided into three distinct groups: *Student* (fulfilling the needs of those taking the Institute's certificate and diploma qualifications); *Professional Development* (for those on formal or self-study vocational training programmes); and *Practitioner* (presented in a more informal, motivating and highly practical manner for the busy marketer).

Formed in 1911, The Chartered Institute of Marketing is now the largest professional marketing management body in Europe with over 24,000 members and 28,000 students located worldwide. Its primary objectives are focused on the development of awareness and understanding of marketing throughout UK industry and commerce and in the raising of standards of professionalism in the education, training and practice of this key business discipline.

Titles in the series

Integrated Marketing Communications

Ian Linton and Kevin Morley

Published on behalf of
The Chartered Institute of Marketing

Butterworth-Heinemann Ltd
Linacre House, Jordan Hill, Oxford OX2 8DP

ℛ A member of the Reed Elsevier plc group

OXFORD   LONDON   BOSTON
MUNICH   NEW DELHI   SINGAPORE   SYDNEY
TOKYO   TORONTO   WELLINGTON

First published 1995
Reprinted 1995

British Library Cataloguing in Publication Data
A catalogue record for this book is available from the British Library

ISBN 0 7506 1938 4

Printed in Great Britain by Clays Ltd, St Ives plc

Contents

Preface

Integrated marketing is attracting advertiser and agency alike. It promises to revolutionize the communications process with a powerful range of business benefits, including creative integrity, consistency of messages, unbiased marketing recommendations, better use of communications media, greater marketing precision, improved operational efficiency, cost savings, high calibre consistent agency service, easier working relations and greater agency accountability.

If you are considering integrated marketing, this book will give you an insight into the practice and the process.

We accept that integrated marketing may not be appropriate for every organization. However, there are a number of important factors that help to indicate the need for integrated marketing.

Your company faces complex issues in the marketplace or your products raise complex issues within the customer company. To market your products or services effectively, you must convince many different decision makers and your communications programme must work consistently across all decision makers.

You are involved in market development projects and it is essential that you carry out market education as well as developing sales. You operate through multiple sales channels and it essential that each one of these operates effectively.

You are introducing new product programmes and you need to convince different groups of people that your products will benefit that organization. Research shows that important decision makers and influencers hold poor perceptions of your organization and it is vital that you reposition the organization.

Limited budgets mean that every element of the programme must work harder and some of the media represent better value for money. You are operating in niche markets and you need to ensure that your marketing performance is consistent across all sectors. Your company is undergoing significant change and you need to ensure that messages are communicated consistently to every member of the target audience. You are introducing a local marketing strategy and you wish to ensure that you offer consistent levels of service and support throughout a network.

If any of these factors apply you should seriously consider integrated marketing.

Ian Linton and Kevin Morley

1 Why integrate?

Introduction

Integrated marketing provides an opportunity to improve the precision and effectiveness of marketing programmes by handling all aspects of marketing through a single source.

An integrated marketing solution uses the most appropriate media and techniques to achieve marketing objectives. There is no 'lead' technique and the solution could include any of the following:

- Advertising
- Direct marketing
- Telemarketing
- Public relations
- Internal communications
- Incentives
- Salesforce communications
- Distributor communications
- Retail support
- Product and technical information
- Corporate identity and corporate communications
- Presentations and exhibitions
- Relationship marketing.

In traditional marketing, many of these activities would be handled by separate specialist agencies or suppliers. The marketing effort is fragmented and the results could be conflicting communications that confuse the customer.

In integrated marketing, all marketing programmes are channelled through a central coordinator and handled by a single agency. The key benefits are:

- Creative integrity
- Consistency of messages
- Unbiased marketing recommendations
- Better use of all media
- Greater marketing precision
- Operational efficiency
- Cost savings
- High calibre consistent service
- Easier working relations
- Greater agency accountability.

This chapter discusses these benefits in more detail and provides initial recommendations for reviewing the potential of integrated marketing and introducing it into a company. Before we look at those benefits, here are two examples of integrated marketing in action.

Integrated marketing in action

Rover Metro

The Metro was launched in 1979, becoming the highest volume seller in Rover's history. The engineering of the car was fundamentally overhauled in 1990, but external appearances were largely unchanged. In 1991, competitive pressure on the Metro increased dramatically with the launch of the Renault Clio and Peugeot 106. Sales share began to fall despite pricing activity.

Integrated marketing agency KMM's first task when they were appointed by Rover in January 1992 was to halt and reverse this decline in share, which had slipped to below 2 per cent. The objective was immediately to lift share to more than 4 per cent with a settled down rate in excess of 3 per cent.

The strategy adopted by KMM was to highlight the changes that had been made to the car in a dramatic and intrusive way, in order to force a reappraisal of a car that most consumers thought they knew. To this end, extensive use was made of an exclusive road test recently conducted by *Car* magazine.

An integrated campaign was developed consisting of forty-second television commercials, 48-sheet posters and a national press campaign featuring a direct response mechanism offering further information. Those who responded to this received their information pack containing a test drive incentive based on the offer of a range of a Harrods merchandise. This promotional offer was also carried through to point-of-sale.

Subsequently, the launch of two new Metro derivatives (a diesel engine and an automatic gearbox) was also handled via direct marketing and point-of-sale. The entire campaign was turned around in eight weeks from receipt of the brief to the TV commercial and first national press ad appearing.

The result of the campaign has been highly satisfactory. Metro's share of the industry volume rose from 1.9 per cent to 4.3 per cent, subsequently settling down to a share in excess of 3.5 per cent. Previously Rover's highest ever response to a test drive incentive programme had been 7000. The integrated campaign, despite the comparatively low profile of the Harrod's offer, generated over 13,500 test drive enquiries.

The total cost of the campaign was under £2.5 million and Rover estimated that the activity boosted profitability by over £7 million. Equally important, image tracking studies show that in several key areas Metro's image has shifted favourably indicating a longer-term benefit from this essentially tactical programme.

Repositioning ICL customer services

When ICL launched a comprehensive range of customer services, they brought together hundreds of services provided by different divisions and business units, each communicating with customers in its way. A complete integrated communications strategy was developed to position ICL as a long-term business partner providing professional services that were vital to achieving the client's business objectives. The programme lasted over two years and a key feature was the inclusion of consistent positioning messages and visual standards in all internal and external service communications. Programme elements included:

- Keynote presentations to explain the strategic importance of services to senior decision makers in business and government
- Customer presentations on ICL's service capability
- Internal presentations to build understanding and awareness of ICL's new direction in services
- Product literature on consultancy, application services, project services, facilities management, managed service, disaster recovery, environmental services and capacity planning services
- Corporate brochures on ICL's services capability
- Salesforce information to explain the importance of selling services to long-term customer loyalty
- Service input to other divisions' product literature
- Services portfolio to help customers select the right service for various business scenarios.

All of these activities were handled by a single agency and the result was consistent presentation of a single integrated communications strategy to all decision makers. The customer service division became the largest single contributor to ICL's total revenue and profit.

Key benefits

Integrated marketing is one of the most exciting developments in marketing. It promises to bring the strengths of above and below the line together and to help marketeers improve the performance of all their sales and marketing campaigns.

Creative integrity

Integrated marketing offers strategic and creative integrity across all media. In practical terms that means the theme and style of advertising is followed consistently through all media. This means a powerful message for the product or service across all above and below the line elements. A company that produces many different campaigns, publications and other marketing support material for a large, complex product range will be able to introduce consistent creative and visual standards. This will enable the company to present a strong unified identity and support all its products and services with powerful branding.

When a consumer gets messages, they should be consistent. In just one campaign, a consumer might view a television commercial, read a press advertisement, receive a direct mail shot, visit a retail outlet where there is point-of-sale material, pick up a product leaflet amd participate in an incentive programme. At the same time the consumer might talk to members of the salesforce, visit an exhibition and receive a call from a telemarketing specialist.

What happens if the creative treatment of each of these is different? Confusion, lack of impact. Does the consumer think they are dealing with the same company? Each of these elements reinforces each other. While it is not essential for the visual and copy treatment to be exactly the same on each element of the campaign, they must be telling the same story. A consistent build-up like this reinforces the impact of the other elements of the programme and helps to move the consumer towards a decision.

In business-to-business marketing, the scenario can be multiplied by the number of people involved in the decision-making process: executive briefing for the senior management team, management guides for departmental managers who might use the product, capability presentations for the buying team, technical literature for technical specialists, product literature for the purchasing department, corporate advertisements and financial public relations aimed at the important influencers, direct marketing to other members of the purchasing team, sales presentations, videos and product proposals. Add the information that distributors and other influencers need in the form of retail advertisements and mailers, point-of-sale material and distributor training and the picture becomes very complex.

What a difference a single integrated campaign can make. While every Rover commercial takes a different creative treatment, they are unified by the line, 'Above all it's a Rover' and information from Rover dealers is reinforced by the line 'above all we're Rover dealers'. Look through Rover literature and you'll find the creative themes echoed in product brochures and at the point-of-sale.

When ICL launched their customer service division, every piece of customer-facing literature and every internal publication contained the same set of core messages, 'Customer services contribute to the improvement of corporate efficiency'. The design treatment featuring computer-generated images was reproduced on product literature, direct marketing, exhibitions, videos, internal communications and retail material. Audiovisual presentations and live presenter scripts echoed the theme that services were strategically important to the customer. Over a three-year period, these messages were reinforced and subtly altered to take account of clients' changing perceptions of the company, but above all reinforcement was the key.

Creative integrity is primarily about managing your customers' perceptions of your products and your business. Research can show how you are perceived in relation to your target perceptions and perceptions of your competitors. This perception should be reinforced in every communication that reaches the customer and prospect. But given the traditional split between above and below the line promotion this is rarely achieved in practice. Accounts are handled by separate agencies, briefed by separate departments and produced by people who want to prove that they are creatively unique. This might produce great work but if it creates confusion in the mind of the consumer, it is creative energy that is wasted.

Sally Line with a modest budget could not hope to take on larger competitors like P&O or Sealink directly in the mainstream media of press and television. But by developing an integrated campaign that reinforced the simple but effective TV themes in direct mail, videos and brochures they are able to hit customers and prospects again and again with the right messages. The reason for the success of the campaign was that it was briefed by a single client to a single agency contact and produced by a single agency team – creative integrity through integrated marketing.

It is worth looking at your own marketing communications material – does it provide customers with consistent messages or does it show that it is produced from different sources?

Consistency of messages

In integrated marketing, all copy is written or edited centrally. Although 'technical' information will vary by product or service, each publication, campaign or marketing communication will include 'positioning' messages which stress generic customer benefits such as quality of service, customer focus, corporate strength and other key factors. This consistency is impossible when copy is produced separately for advertisements, direct mail, product literature – all aimed at the same customer. Integrated marketing will ensure that every form of customer contact reinforces the customer's positive perception of the company.

Like creative integrity, consistency is a major benefit of integrated marketing. It is a sad fact that professional copywriters rarely stray beyond the safe bounds of an advertisement, mail shot or corporate brochure. Yet these are just a small element of the communications that hit customers and prospects every day. There is a vast amount of material – product literature, product guides, sales training programmes, audiovisual presentations, internal communications and single direct marketing material, technical literature and capability presentations – that is used to move the client along the decision-making process. These are the neglected areas of marketing communications yet they have a significant input on the client's perceptions of products and customers. Integrated marketing ensures that each of these media is treated as an important marketing tool and receives the same standard of professional treatment.

One of the easiest ways to do that is to ensure that consistent messages are included in each publication. Consistent messages enable you to keep repeating the positioning messages that are crucial to long-term perception management and to incorporate the specific targeted messages that are needed for individual members of the purchasing team. To make the most of this benefit it is essential that a key message programme is developed.

Visual standards also help to reinforce the consistency of integrated communications. By imposing corporate design standards on all promotional material and utilizing key visual elements on advertisements and all other communications material, the visual identity can be reinforced. A corporate identity is a major investment for any company but it pays for itself in increased recognition and stronger perceptions. Integrated marketing reinforces the benefits of a corporate identity programme by applying it to all media and ensuring that the company is immediately recognized. Different products, different campaigns, information from separate divisions can all be coordinated by introducing consistent messages.

Unbiased recommendations

In integrated marketing, one agency should handle all aspects of marketing and operate 'through the line'. An agency that works through the line has no bias towards any in particular of the media: they are all treated with the same attention because an integrated agency does not have to worry about earning commission. This means that the agency is able to recommend the most appropriate strategy which might include direct marketing, incentives or sales support for distributors and agents.

If you approached an advertising agency or public relations consultancy, you would probably be surprised if they did not recommend media advertising or a public relations campaign. If you briefed a design consultancy on your communications requirements, the chances are that you would be operating a print-based programme. The more specific the supplier the more likely you are to get a predictable response. This is not a criticism because it is the role of a specialist to provide a specialist service. But where do you turn to for unbiased advice on the best mix of media to achieve communications and business objectives?

While a number of major agencies have set up below the line subsidiaries, ostensibly to provide the client with a complete service, these below the line activities are inevitably secondary to the main business of producing advertisements. The system produces great advertisements – no one would deny that – but the system does not help the client whose needs are more diverse. In an integrated strategy you need to know that every element of the marketing mix is working hard and contributing to the overall success of the campaign. Advertisements, for example, may fail to reach the key decision makers for your product. Salesforce contact may be vital to securing a major contract. An extended video could provide a vital live action demonstration of your product and give your direct salesforce an important training tool. The success of your campaign may depend on effective local marketing by a distributor network or you may have a high awareness but low levels of repeat business and you wish to improve long-term relationships with your customers.

You may be aware of these requirements, but if you want unbiased advice on how to achieve them where would you turn to? An integrated marketing agency handles the full range of communications tasks and is in a unique position to offer you unbiased advice on the solution that is best for your business. Above all the agency is accountable for the success of your business. If it does not produce the results then it has failed and, while the wrong recommendations may yield a short-term profit, in the long term they could lose a client and that is something no agency wishes to do. An integrated marketing agency is looking for partnership and that means giving you the best advice on achieving your business objectives.

Direct marketing is one of the most important elements in an integrated marketing campaign – it can produce effective results in its own right as an advertising medium, but it also plays an essential support role to other media and therefore offers both agency and client considerable flexibility. This level of unbiased recommendation is vital for clients who have a limited budget or who face complex marketing tasks which require efficient performance across all media.

Better use of all media

In integrated marketing different techniques and media are used to support each other to improve overall marketing effectiveness. For example:

- Direct marketing and telemarketing are used to support direct response advertising campaigns
- Selected customer incentives are used to increase response to advertising or direct marketing campaigns
- Relationship marketing programmes are used to increase customer retention
- Sales training, targeted incentive programmes and direct marketing are used to improve direct sales performance.

By integrating these activities, it is possible to increase response rates and improve the overall effectiveness of marketing. As an example, three computer companies who integrated their direct marketing programmes with telemarketing increased response rates by between 10 and 18 per cent.

Integrated marketing ensures that you get the best from each medium. An exhibition specialist, for example, would be in the best position to produce a high quality exhibition stand but may not have the resources or the experience to supply all the back-up services that are needed to make the exhibition successful. For example, direct marketing of invitations to delegates and follow-up by telephone of all attendees can help to reinforce the work that was done on the stand. Incentives during the exhibition and suitable exhibition literature can all help to make the expenditure work much harder.

A seminar which is integrated with an executive briefing programme and a direct marketing campaign which provides senior executives with useful product and service management guides ensures that clients get full benefit from the seminar programme and that the overall communications effect is much stronger. By integrating public relations with advertising and using telemarketing to follow up all direct marketing campaigns, the impact and effectiveness of every campaign can be increased. IBM in the USA found that adding telemarketing to direct marketing increased response levels from 1 per cent to around 19 per cent – a dramatic increase and an excellent advertisement for the power of integrated marketing.

Perhaps the core of the integrated marketing strategy is the database because this makes every other element of the marketing mix work that much harder. The database can be built up from the response to advertisements and can then be used to supplement the advertising campaign by directly targeting those people who cannot be reached by conventional media. Telemarketing uses the database as a method of qualifying prospects, direct selling and building long-term relationships with customers. The database is also useful for developing precisely targeted direct marketing campaigns that ensure that every element of the programme is used to its full extent.

Greater marketing precision

Integrated marketing contributes to greater marketing precision. Media advertising has traditionally had the highest profile of all marketing activities and attracted the greatest talent. While media planning, for example, has become extremely sophisticated, it remains essentially a broadcast marketing skill. In an integrated marketing programme, direct mail and other precision marketing tools are used extensively to achieve specific communications objectives. For example, a programme which requires consistent nationwide retail performance must include local marketing activities – product training for distributors, retail support programmes, local advertising and staff incentives to ensure commitment. Provided they are given professional support within an integrated marketing programme, they will be able to be used to achieve specific measurable objectives.

Integrated marketing makes extensive use of database marketing techniques: information from direct response advertising, direct marketing campaigns and telemarketing is used to build a customer and prospect database. This database enables a company to build up a comprehensive picture of individual customers and prospects so that future marketing programmes are focused with great precision.

Direct marketing can be used to supplement broadcast media across the spectrum. As Chapter 2 shows, direct marketing can be used in a wide variety of support roles, each of them adding greater precision to other media. In the example given, direct mail is used to generate leads, follow up advertisement enquiries, build relationships with customers, reach prospects or decision makers who are not accessible by conventional methods and supplement promotional and incentive programmes. Because direct marketing is such a precise medium, it means that any element of the campaign can be fine tuned to be targeted precisely.

A single media strategy may be concentrated on a key part of the target but it runs the risk of missing the important prospects and attempting to do everything. Integrated marketing allows you to concentrate on your mainstream marketing programmes while introducing niche market programmes and focusing on specific elements of the marketing mix to win key prospects. Both broadcast and targeted media will be handled at the same professional level.

Operational efficiency

Another major benefit of integrated marketing is operational efficiency. It takes fewer people to manage integrated marketing. There is a single interface with one agency which ties up less management and administrative time. Because there is a single interface there is no inter-agency conflict of interest. When different departments or individuals are working with separate specialist agencies, there is little coordination and a great deal of duplication of effort. Agency and supplier management costs are duplicated because each agency/client relationship requires separate estimating, ordering, invoicing and other control procedures.

At its simplest one client deals with one agency contact. An integrated campaign is produced by an agency and the client receives a single itemized invoice. Single-source service is also becoming prevalent in other areas of business such as computer services where a single lead supplier coordinates the client's entire requirements and improves operational efficiency.

Compare the simplicity of an integrated marketing relationship with the traditional structures of client, agencies and specialist suppliers. In a large fmcg company you might find brand managers dealing with different advertising agencies, a marketing director working with another agency on corporate campaigns, incentives and promotions specialists using groups of suppliers, publications managers dealing with designers, writers, typesetters and printers to produce product literature and point-of-sale, training managers producing marketing information for the salesforce, national account managers producing programmes for individual retail outlets, public affairs executives handling press and public relations activities through public relations consultancies, a design manager developing a new corporate identity and a direct mail specialist to produce consumer direct marketing campaigns. If they and their agencies all have personal ambitions, the chances are that integration will be non-existent. Everyone will be going their own way and the results could be both visual chaos and an administrative nightmare. Each department or individual will be selecting and monitoring suppliers operating to their own standards, raising purchase orders, checking invoices and creating payment authorization. This is time-consuming and inefficient. It takes up a great deal of management time and it can lead to duplication.

In an integrated marketing situation, a single agency is appointed to handle and coordinate all marketing and communications activities. While they may not handle every type of work with their own resources, they also provide a management service to deal with specialist suppliers, selecting them, briefing them, evaluating their work and handling all administration on behalf of the client. By channelling all agency/client communications through a single point of contact, there is a considerable saving in management time and avoidance of duplication. The key benefits of integrated marketing in this area are:

- Single point of contact
- Simplified administration
- Consistency of standards applied to all suppliers
- Single invoice
- Reduction in management administration time
- Greater control over creative standards.

Cost savings

Integrated marketing saves money – the previous section outlined the hidden cost savings of simplifying the account management process. Apart from the reduction in administration costs, there is also a potential headcount saving. People who have been used to handling routine management and administration of routine client/agency relationships can be redeployed to carry out more productive tasks. In a major organization, the headcount saving can be significant and this means better use of your own resources. But the savings are not limited to administration – consolidating all expenditure in a single agency should mean greater value for money.

The Metro case history demonstrates a saving of around 10 per cent compared with multiple sourcing. There are direct savings on production/media costs, plus indirect savings on administration and management. That means budgets can go further and work harder to support the bottom line. Key savings include:

- Better media rates through centralized buying
- Rationalization of product literature
- Elimination of duplication in areas such as photography
- Reduction in hidden internal administrative costs
- Competitive centralized buying across all marketing activities.

The benefits of centralized media buying through media independents and full-service agencies have already been well established. Integrated marketing takes it a stage further and ensures that all media are purchased centrally so the client gets the benefit not only of efficient press, television and radio buying but also benefits from volume buying of print, artwork and other specialist marketing services. Integrated marketing agencies are able to select the most efficient cost-effective suppliers and work in long-term partnership with them. Partnership and continuity of work mean that the supplier can afford to offer more competitive prices and better value for money.

Many integrated marketing agencies utilize BS 5750 quality standards to manage the quality of their suppliers and their internal processes. This not only improves quality, but can also help to reduce the cost of waste – that can be a significant saving.

Integrated marketing reduces a great deal of duplication in the creative and production processes. To take a simple example, photography can be planned in advance to ensure maximum utilization of location and material. Take a car manufacturer, for example. Photography would be required for press and television advertisements, videos, product literature, direct mail, point-of-sale, training material and distributor support programmes. If each of these specialist departments or agencies organized their own photography, there would be an enormous element of wastage, not to mention creative disparity. Integrated marketing ensures that creative resources like this can be utilized in the most cost-effective way.

The development of creative treatment could yield further cost savings. As the first section showed, creative integrity is an essential element of integrated marketing: this means that the creative themes are developed centrally and then fine-tuned to the specific needs of each of the media. Depending on the method of agency remuneration, this can represent a significant saving on production costs over a complete campaign and reduce the potential duplication of work.

High calibre service

When a single agency is working across all media, there is a consistency of service which is not normally found in below the line activities. The same creative teams work on all communications programmes and any specialist services bought in by the agency are quality controlled to provide consistent standards.

Because of the traditional divide between above and below the line media, there has been an inconsistency of service that has left below the line clients struggling. Historically, below the line services have been provided by specialist suppliers reacting to specific client briefs and there has been no continuity in the relationship or the quality of work. Publications and promotional projects were often decided on the basis of price guides rather than quality of recommendations. Publications were treated as a series of one-off projects and the supplier as only as good as the last job. Brochures were produced on demand and this gave the supplier no opportunity or incentive to develop a better understanding of the client's business.

Compare this with advertising or public relations where agencies and consultancies are given a long-term contract and a budget to achieve specific results. The agencies are not quoting on a job-by-job basis and they are expected to produce campaigns that achieve long-term results.

Integrated marketing ensures that above and below the line activities are both treated with the same professionalism. Below the line activities are integrated into the overall strategy and they are created by the same teams that produce the above the line material. This is where the consistency becomes more obvious. In agencies that handle below the line in a conventional way, top teams worked on the national press and television campaigns – the high profile accounts that everyone welcomes – but trade advertisements, brochures, local marketing support material and other below the line material was given to junior teams who had to get their hands dirty. The result was second division work for first division clients. If the below the line work was handled outside the main agency, there was little opportunity to control creative standards because the work was handled by different creative groups and each was issuing their own version of creative standards. But, with integrated marketing, the creative standards are controlled by the coordinating group and the detailed implementation may be handled by outside groups.

Easier working relationships

By dealing with a single agency the problems of coordination and project management are simplified. It is the integrated marketing agency's responsibility to coordinate all activities and specialist suppliers. Because an agency has grasped the fundamentals of the client's business on one of the media, there is no new learning curve when it comes to working on different media. A new project in a different medium can be turned around quickly.

Integrated marketing provides a single source of contact between agency and client – ideally this should be one of client and one agency contact, although politics may dictate that there are other contacts on the client side. On the agency side there is a single account director whose role is to coordinate all activities and ensure that all the specialists work to the same high standards. This simplifies administration and agency management. The client deals with one contact for all requirements and can ensure that everyone is provided with a brief to a consistently high standard. The agency can plan complete above and below the line accounts in one session and introduce priorities into the work. The creative teams do not have to relearn the visual and creative standards for each project.

Agency accountability

Integrated marketing increases agency accountability. Because one agency is handling all aspects of marketing, the agency is in an ideal position to recommend the most effective solution.

Any agency which handles every aspect of marketing is completely accountable for marketing performance. When the Rover 600 was launched, KMM was totally accountable for its performance. They achieved target market share and reduced the overall cost of the campaign. In an integrated marketing agency, everything is under the agency's control. A conventional agency could argue that it is only responsible for part of the marketing programme and that success depends on many different factors. However, an agency that controls all the factors has nowhere to hide and cannot blame anyone else. It cannot use the excuse that other elements of the marketing mix are outside its control. Agency performance should be measurable and that increases value for money.

Reviewing the potential

Integrated marketing offers powerful creative and cost benefits but it must be carefully evaluated before making a commitment to a single agency/single solution. These are some of the indicators that demonstrate the need for an integrated approach:

- Customers receive communications material from different sources in the same company.
- Different company departments commission their own marketing material.
- Visual and copy standards vary between departments.
- The company is losing the opportunity to cross-sell and build long-term relationships with customers.
- The company uses many different suppliers to produce marketing support material and there is little co-ordination between suppliers.
- Visual standards do not result in consistency.
- The company uses many different sales channels to market its products and channel performance varies considerably.
- The cost of marketing administration is high because of the number of different suppliers.
- Staff currently spending time on producing marketing support material could be better utilized on more productive customer-focused tasks.

If these factors apply, a company should carry out a more detailed feasibility study to identify the most important areas for improvement.

Introducing an integrated marketing programme

These are the key stages in introducing integrated marketing into an organization:

- Establish the right internal structure
- Select a suitable agency to handle integrated marketing
- Select pilot projects or campaigns to evaluate the potential for integrated marketing.

Internal structure for integrated marketing

The client can simplify the structure of their marketing department. There should be one coordinator or coordinating group working with one contact with the agency: this ensures that the agency is briefed clearly on every aspect of the communications programme.

Most clients who adopt integrated marketing find that they can reduce the number of people involved in the marketing support process. The management of suppliers is handled by staff within the agency and their costs can be apportioned across a number of different accounts.

The marketing director is likely to be the key person in the briefing process. It is his or her responsibility to determine the overall strategy and to coordinate the requirements of functional specialists. For example, within a company there might be a number of executives responsible for different aspects of the marketing programme:

- Marketing director
- Sales director
- Customer service director
- Distributor operations director.

There might also be marketing services specialists responsible for:

- Consumer advertising
- Product information
- Retail advertising
- Sales promotion
- Public affairs
- Event management
- Direct marketing.

If each of these specialists has been acting on his own initiative, there is a considerable duplication of effort:

- Establishing and managing relations with suppliers
- Administering supplier business
- Developing a brief and a creative strategy
- Monitoring quality
- Coordinating marketing activities with other specialists.

It is not possible, at this stage, to make detailed recommendations on a rationalization process, but the general principle is that all work should be channelled through a central group or individual.

Selecting an agency

Integrated marketing means that one agency handles all creative work and coordinates the work of other marketing specialists. These are the key factors in selecting an integrated marketing agency:

- The agency employs high calibre staff in all the key marketing disciplines.
- The agency has quality-controlled suppliers to maintain consistent standards across all media.
- The agency has the financial stability to maintain a presence for the long term.
- The agency can demonstrate a successful track record in each of the key media.
- The agency can measure the marketing and financial performance of their campaigns.

Within the agency, the core team is:

- Planner
- Creative director
- Account director.

They have access to a range of specialists in each of the marketing disciplines. The account directors are the key players because they liaise with the client marketing director and interpret the client brief to the rest of the team.

The agency is used to working with a wide variety of suppliers so is in a position to select the most appropriate for the project. The client is likely to have a more limited choice. Specialist suppliers work on a partnership basis with the agency, meeting their quality requirements and operating within a consistent strategic brief. BS 5750 has a useful role to play in maintaining an effective relationship between supplier and agency.

This close working relationship helps to maintain consistent quality visual standards. Suppliers are managed at a creative and strategic level, while the detailed project implementation is carried out by specialists who understand the practicalities of print, direct mail or events. By working closely with an agency, a supplier builds a better understanding of the project and quality requirements. This ensures a continuity of service.

The client/agency relationship

This needs to be a long-term relationship so that:

- The agency gets to know the client's business thoroughly
- The client adjusts to dealing with a single source of supply
- The agency performance can be measured effectively
- Client and agency understand the other variables in the success of a marketing programme
- The client retains the key role in developing marketing strategy but can spend less time in managing supplier relationships.

Pilot projects

Integrated marketing can involve major changes in the way a company organizes and operates its marketing programmes. It should therefore carry out a number of pilot projects before moving into full-scale integration. Pilot projects can cover:

- Single product
- Single campaign.

In the project, all the appropriate media are used and the campaign results are measured. When the pilot projects have been completed, the company can then introduce a phased programme of change to full integration.

Summary

Integrated marketing provides a powerful range of business benefits, including creative integrity, consistency of messages, unbiased marketing recommendations, better use of communications media, greater marketing precision, improved operational efficiency, cost savings, high calibre consistent agency service, easier working relations and greater agency accountability. However, introducing integrated marketing represents a considerable risk and it is important to review its potential and implications before committing to a single-source solution. Solving internal political problems, selecting the right agency and operating pilot programmes are important stages in a successful transition to integrated marketing.

2 Building blocks

Introduction

This chapter outlines the key elements or 'building blocks' of integrated marketing and shows how they relate to each other. It is fundamental to integrated marketing that you do not treat these elements as separate activities, but use them as a series of interrelated marketing tools which support each other. Although campaigns take many different forms, there are core elements that are integral to the successful development of an integrated marketing strategy. The most important of these are:

- Advertising
- Direct marketing
- Telemarketing
- Press information
- Internal communications
- Sales promotion and incentives
- Salesforce communications
- Distributor communications
- Retail support
- Product and technical information
- Corporate identity and corporate communications
- Presentations and exhibitions
- Relationship marketing.

Traditional marketing methods treat different elements as separate unrelated entities, each of which might produce incremental results. The objectives and schedule for each of the elements is set separately and the programmes may be handled by separate departments who work with different agencies. This can lead to fragmentation and dilution of overall effectiveness:

- Different messages
- Different creative treatment
- Timing problems
- Dilution of visual standards.

In the integrated approach, the elements support each other. For example, an advertising campaign with reply coupon is integrated with a direct mail programme which is followed up by telemarketing. Without the support of the other marketing elements, the advertising and direct mail programmes would each have achieved results but together they reinforce each other to achieve real impact.

Because budgets vary from client to client, we have shown how each of the elements can be used in a 'standalone' role and as part of an integrated campaign. This gives you greater flexibility in selecting the media that are most appropriate to achieving your campaign objectives.

Using building blocks in a campaign

In this chapter we look at the building blocks, not in isolation, but in relationship to each other. Each building block is considered as part of a continuous process and the individual sections show how each building block contributes to the success of the overall campaign. To demonstrate the process, we have used the building blocks as part of a fictitious campaign to launch a new car insurance policy.

The insurance policy will be based on a telephone handling system and will be marketed through financial intermediaries and direct to the consumer. The proposition to the consumer is that the process of taking out a policy and making a claim is quicker and simpler. The company does not have sufficient budget to set up a direct consumer sales operation in competition with the major players in the market; it therefore relies on building up a strong local 'distributor' network of financial intermediaries. The programme must balance consumer and distributor marketing.

Advertising

Advertising is a logical starting point for a campaign like this. Insurance companies are significant advertisers in the press, on television and radio, and in specialist consumer and professional finance publications. This product is aimed at a broad base of consumers, rather than niche markets, and the company aims to win business from competitors who offer a similar telephone-based service.

Consumer advertising options

Consumer advertising would enable the company to reach prospects efficiently, provided the budget was adequate. The following media would be appropriate:

- National and regional daily and Sunday newspapers with a personal finance section
- National and regional daily and Sunday newspapers with a motoring section
- Local daily or weekly newspapers, particularly those with a motoring or personal finance section
- National or local commercial radio stations
- Network or regional television
- Specialist personal finance publications such as *Moneywise* or the customer publications of banks, building societies or credit card operators
- Special interest car magazines.

Advertising options to reach professional advisers

Advertising might also be used to reach the financial intermediaries who would carry out local marketing of the product. *British Rate and Data* (BRAD) lists a number of professional publications in its insurance section, including:

- *Brokers Monthly*
- *The Broker*
- *Insurance Age.*

Financial intermediaries could also be reached through the personal finance pages of national and regional daily or Sunday newspapers.

Advertising in a stand-alone role

With an adequate budget and effective media planning, it would be possible to use advertising alone to launch and market the new product. In this situation, advertising would have a number of objectives:

- Raise consumer awareness of the new product
- Raise professional awareness of the new product
- Explain the comparative benefits of the product
- Generate initial requests for quotations
- Sustain levels of requests for quotations over a period of time.

The success of the launch would be directly related to the size and efficient use of the budget, and a company with a smaller budget would be unlikely to compete effectively with larger insurance companies. However, by integrating advertising with other marketing activities, the company can use advertising for specific tasks within the overall programme and make more effective use of its budget.

Advertising in an integrated programme

In an integrated programme, advertising is just one of the marketing tools available, and it can be used in the most efficient way. In the insurance campaign, advertising can be used in a number of different ways:

- As a national direct response medium to generate leads for a corporate direct marketing or telemarketing campaign
- As a local direct response medium to generate leads for local follow up by financial intermediaries
- As part of a selective regional sales promotion campaign that offers prospects incentives for providing database information
- As a local or regional joint campaign between the insurance company and selected financial intermediaries
- As part of a national or regional consumer awareness campaign, with different weights of support to selected regions. This approach could also be used in test marketing
- As part of a campaign to improve the level of local representation in selected regions. The insurance company could offer advertising as part of its local support package.

These options mean that advertising now becomes a much more flexible medium: it does not have to carry the whole burden of 'shifting the product' and it can be used where it is most effective.

Direct marketing

Direct marketing is one of the most flexible tools in an integrated marketing programme. It can be used to reinforce the effectiveness of other marketing tools or it can be used alone in a variety of different ways. Direct mail advertising, for example, can be a viable alternative to press or broadcast media and it can be used to reach specific sectors of the market. In an integrated campaign, it can also be used to follow up prospects who request further information and it can be used to maintain effective contact and build long-term relationships with customers.

Consumer direct marketing options

Direct marketing could be used to support the consumer marketing programme in a number of different ways. Its effectiveness would not be restricted by budget:

- Sending new product information to existing company car policy holders
- Sending new product information to other company policy holders
- Sending new product information to lapsed policy holders
- Sending targeted information to specific types of existing policy holder
- Sending information to a database of prospects generated through consumer advertising
- Sending information to a database of prospects compiled by local financial intermediaries
- Sending information to a database of prospects generated by other methods.

By comparing direct marketing in relation to other broadcast media, you can determine the most effective route for reaching new prospects. Direct marketing also allows you to approach new prospects in a variety of different ways, using different creative approaches or varying the promotional offer. The insurance company planned a diverse direct marketing campaign which included the following elements:

- A series of special offers targeted at the age and lifestyle of the recipient:
  - Young drivers were offered discounts on car audio systems and information on autosport
  - Family motorists were offered discounts on car security systems or membership of a motoring organization
- Holiday breaks were offered to customers who replied within a certain timescale
- Follow-up mailings to customers who had not responded within a certain timescale
- Welcome mailings to prospects who responded or opened a policy.

After the critical launch period, direct marketing can be used as part of a relationship marketing programme; this is discussed in more detail later in the chapter.

Direct marketing options to reach professional advisers

Financial intermediaries are a clearly identifiable group who can be easily reached through direct marketing. However, given the volume of direct mail that they are likely to receive, direct marketing must be used carefully to achieve real impact – a new policy launch could easily be lost in the weight of product information that they receive. The insurance company has a number of options:

- A special launch pack with incentives, aimed at all intermediaries
- A launch pack marketed on a regional basis
- A launch pack test marketed through selected intermediaries.

Like the consumer direct marketing programme, the launch programme can be varied with different incentives and offers to evaluate the effectiveness of different approaches.

Direct marketing in an integrated programme

Direct marketing can be used in a standalone role as an alternative to broadcast media, but in an integrated campaign it must be used to strengthen the overall effectiveness of the campaign. As a first stage, the direct marketing programme can be integrated with both the consumer and the financial intermediary advertising campaigns.

In the consumer campaign, it could be used in the following ways:

- As a follow-up to the direct response advertising campaign. The advertisements provide information on warm prospects which can be used to form a database for future direct marketing programmes.
- To make differentiated offers to prospects who respond to the advertising campaign.
- To supplement the advertising campaign's coverage of different target markets. Direct marketing can be used to reach sectors that cannot be reached efficiently by other media or to provide increased reach or frequency.
- To reinforce the impact of the advertising campaign by selective follow-up.

This is just one aspect of integration and it shows how advertising and direct marketing can together achieve higher impact or improve conversion ratios.

Telemarketing

Telemarketing can be used to supplement the advertising and direct marketing campaigns through inbound and outbound programmes.

Outbound programmes

Outbound programmes are those in which the company takes the initiative. It can be used to handle a number of different tasks:

- Direct sales to prospects over the telephone
- Acquiring new financial intermediaries or keeping current advisers up-to-date with new products
- Maintaining contact with current customers and using the relationship to launch new products
- Generating leads from unqualified mailing lists and following up direct marketing programmes
- Winning back lapsed customers by introducing them to new products which may be of greater interest
- Following up leads generated through advertising or direct marketing or via financial intermediaries
- Carrying out market research using the surveys to establish consumer response to the products or to sales incentives
- Maintaining contact with both consumers and financial intermediaries as part of a relationship marketing programme.

Inbound programmes

In inbound telemarketing, the prospect or customer calls the company in response to an offer or to get further information. In a campaign like this, the insurance company would offer consumers a freephone number that makes it easier to respond. It is vital that these calls are answered professionally by people with the experience and knowledge to deal with queries at many different levels.

Inbound telemarketing can be used in a number of ways in the context of this campaign:

- To provide a point of response for queries generated through advertising or direct marketing campaigns
- To obtain information from respondents as a basis for future database marketing
- To demonstrate high levels of customer service.

Telemarketing in an integrated campaign

As we explained at the beginning of this section, telemarketing can be used as a direct sales tool, especially to existing and lapsed customers. However, using telemarketing in conjunction with other marketing techniques can contribute to better response and conversion ratios. An American direct marketing magazine reported significant improvements in response rates using integrated techniques:

- Hewlett-Packard increased from 1.5 per cent to 12 per cent response
- AT&T increased from 1 per cent to 11 per cent response
- IBM increased from 1 per cent to 19 per cent response.

While the author made the point that this level of increase is unlikely to be general and there may be other contributory factors, the examples demonstrate that integration works. Telemarketing can be integrated with other campaign elements in the following ways:

- Following up leads generated through advertising or direct marketing
- Following up targeted direct marketing campaigns to specific sectors of the market with differentiated offers
- Carrying out joint direct marketing/telemarketing campaigns in conjunction with local financial intermediaries
- Pre-testing campaigns or concepts before operating the campaign.

In an integrated campaign, telemarketing can add an important dimension to the launch programme.

Press information

Like advertising, press information enables the insurance to reach both prospects and professional advisers. However, press information is not trying to generate direct response; it builds awareness and recognition of the insurance company and helps prospects to differentiate its services from those of its competitors.

For the sake of illustration, a consumer press information would use the same media as the advertising campaign:

- National and regional daily and Sunday newspapers with a personal finance section
- National and regional daily and Sunday newspapers with a motoring section
- Local daily or weekly newspapers, particularly those with a motoring or personal finance section
- National or local commercial radio stations
- Network or regional television
- Specialist personal finance publications such as *Moneywise* or the customer publications of banks, building societies or credit card operators
- Special interest car magazines.

Press information might also be used to reach the financial inter-mediaries who would carry out local marketing of the product. The advertising media are appropriate for the press information programme, including:

- *Brokers Monthly*
- *The Broker*
- *Insurance Age*
- Personal finance pages of national and regional daily or Sunday newspapers.

Press information in a standalone role

Press information can be used to support the launch and marketing of the new product. The press information programme would have a number of objectives:

- Raise consumer awareness of the new product
- Raise professional awareness of the new product
- Explain the comparative benefits of the product
- Raise awareness of the company.

The press information could take the form of product press releases, feature articles on trends in the insurance industry, interviews or comments from key members of staff, contributions to product reviews, or editorial supporting reader competitions.

Press relations in an integrated programme

Press activities could also be used in the context of a wider public relations campaign. Sponsorship of sporting or entertainment events, for example, can increase awareness and build a high profile for the company, leaving advertising and direct marketing to focus on direct response and brand-building strategies. In the insurance campaign, press information can be used in a number of different ways:

- As part of a national or regional consumer awareness campaign, in conjunction with advertising and direct marketing
- As part of a selective regional sales promotion campaign that offers prospects incentives for providing database informa-tion – for example a reader competition run in conjunction with a newspaper or magazine
- As a local or regional joint campaign between the insurance company and selected financial intermediaries

In business-to-business markets, the role of press information is extremely important and it is an essential element in an integrated campaign. The specialist business-to-business press provides highly efficient media for reaching specific members of a target audience. For example, an integrated campaign for a capital equipment manufacturer might utilize product press information in vertical market publications to reach technical specialists, feature articles in senior management magazines to raise corporate awareness, and contributions to industry surveys in business magazines to reach other members of a purchasing team.

Internal communications

Internal communications is one of the most neglected areas of communications. Companies who spend large budgets on client communications neglect one of the most important media – their staff. Staff who do not understand customer needs are unlikely to deliver the highest standards of customer service, and if they do not understand the benefits of your products and services they will not be able to take full advantage of marketing opportunities.

Internal communications must form part of an integrated marketing communications programme from the start. It is not essential that every member of staff is fully aware of every marketing activity – there are key customer-facing staff who are crucial to the process. In the insurance company these would include:

- Customer service staff
- Telemarketing specialists
- Product specialists
- Marketing staff
- Sales support staff
- Claims handling staff.

Communications with sales staff and financial advisers is an essential part of internal communications but is considered in more detail later in this section. Effective internal communications provide a number of important business benefits in an integrated marketing campaign:

- Ensure that staff understand the importance of customer service
- Ensure that customer-facing staff understand products so that they can present benefits to customers effectively
- Ensure that staff have all the information they need to handle sales queries

- Encourage support staff to give their full commitment to customer-facing staff
- Ensure that staff understand the reasons for any programme change needed to improve levels of customer service
- Ensure that senior executives and departmental managers commit adequate resources to provide the right levels of service.

Internal communications in the insurance company takes a number of forms:

- Presentations and videos to introduce the concept and implications of customer service programmes
- Employee magazines that keep staff up-to-date with developments
- Briefing meetings to review progress and tackle specific projects
- Incentive and motivation programmes to ensure that staff are focused on high standards for customer service.

Internal communications should not be neglected because it ensures that staff respond effectively to enquiries generated by other integrated marketing activities.

Sales promotion and incentives

Sales promotion and incentives can be used at two levels in an integrated marketing programme:

- Tactically to improve response rates or build traffic
- Strategically to support long-term branding and build customer loyalty.

It is important to utilize both aspects because sales promotion is often regarded as simply tactical.

Tactical consumer promotion

Sales promotion can be integrated with advertising and direct marketing campaigns to raise response rates for both initial enquiries and conversions, for example including a group of special offers which encourage initial enquiry, signing an agreement and paying the first premium. The sales promotion offers help to move the consumer to action and are an integral part of a response programme. They can be used in the following ways:

- To support lead generation programmes for direct marketing and telemarketing
- To encourage prospects to provide database information
- In a test marketing programme to assess the effectiveness of different media and promotional combinations
- Encouraging prospects to commit to purchase in a direct response programme
- To target different groups of consumers with special offers that reflect different lifestyles. The section on direct marketing gave examples of targeted offers for young drivers and family motorists that formed an integral part of the direct marketing programme.

The same types of tactical promotion can be used to support local marketing to financial advisers:

- Special offers tailored to local market conditions
- Targeted promotions with selected intermediaries.

In both cases the promotions would be used to support lead generation and direct sales.

Strategic sales promotion

Strategic sales promotion can be integrated with relationship marketing programmes to support branding opportunities and build customer loyalty. For example, special offers can be developed to encourage existing policy holders to trade up to higher value policies or to try other products in the group. A strategic campaign can operate in a number of ways:

- Offering customers and prospects special services or other offers that support core brand qualities
- Rewarding existing customers for renewal and repeat business
- Using strategic promotions to reactivate lapsed accounts
- Offering customers high quality incentives to support the marketing of higher value products
- Structuring programmes to suit different customer spending levels.

Strategic sales promotion and incentive programmes can play a valuable role in supporting other marketing activities.

Incentive programmes

Incentive programmes can be used to focus the salesforce and financial advisers on important marketing activities. Sales incentives should be directly related to the current campaigns and can be both tactical and strategic. Tactical incentives could include:

- Product sales incentives based on new business generation and policy sales, with a structured scheme related to the number of conversions. This would ensure that the salesforce made the best use of the leads generated through direct marketing and advertising and concentrated on building higher levels of new sales.
- Structured incentives for target market sales. If the company wants to increase penetration in specific sectors, tie the incentive programme to sales in niche markets and integrate direct marketing and telemarketing activity to increase the chances of success.
- Short-term incentives to achieve revenue targets.
- Incentives linked to generation of database information, even though the prospect may not purchase immediately.

These short-term incentives help to focus the salesforce on immediate goals so that they can maintain high levels of sales.

Strategic incentives can help to reduce the salesforce effort over the long term. Customer relationships and high levels of repeat business are critical to the future development of the company and this will require a changing emphasis in the salesforce. The salesforce will be responsible for identifying customer needs and working as consultants rather than selling specific products. The emphasis is on looking at the customer's overall financial requirements so frequent meetings and regular communications are an important part of the process. The calls may not result in immediate sales and this would affect salesforce earning potential. The incentive scheme should reflect this changing role and could include the following elements:

- Structured incentives linked to overall customer performance rather than short-term sales.
- Incentives linked to training achievement – the training would reflect the new skills of consultancy and relationship marketing which now become more important.

- Structured incentives linked to high levels of customer retention and repeat business – this helps to change the emphasis from new business at all costs to protection of the business. It represents a change in role from hunter to farmer and it is important to reward the salesforce for their contribution to the success of the programme.

A strategic incentive programme like that would be integrated with a relationship marketing programme, customer promotional activities that reflect customer retention and a change in the corporate communications programme that reflected the changing relationship between the insurance company and its customers.

Strategic incentive programmes can also be used to improve relationships with financial advisers and other non-franchised sales agents. Incentives would be used to encourage them to recommend the company's products and to focus on prospects and market sectors in line with the company's own objectives. An incentive programme would include elements such as:

- Incentives for signing up as an agent of the company. The incentive programme would be integrated with direct marketing and national or regional advertising campaigns designed to raise the profile of the insurance company in the professional sector and recruit new agents.
- Incentives linked to the level of business generated on behalf of the insurance company. The programme would be integrated with joint marketing support programmes that enabled the advisers to achieve a higher profile in their own local market.
- Incentive programmes that rewarded the adviser with business systems or programmes that strengthened the relationship between insurance companies and advisers.

This type of incentive programme is designed to build closer relations with financial advisers as well as building sales. It is therefore an integral part of an overall campaign to improve levels of service and contact with the customer by making best use of direct and indirect channels.

Salesforce communications

Incentive programmes are just one of the elements that can be used to achieve the best performance from the salesforce. Ongoing salesforce communications are essential to ensure that they are always up-to-date with developments and committed to making the most of the marketing opportunities available. The salesforce can be the most important point of contact with the customer and it is vital that they are fully aware of all the support that is available to them. Salesforce communications can take a number of forms:

- Briefings and meetings such as sales conferences, regional business meetings, product launches.
- Regular business bulletins covering product and market information, business opportunities, competitive updates and company news.
- Salesforce briefing material on new products or special markets – these would include benefits of the product, market characteristics, sales guides, marketing support and incentive programmes related to the launch, targets and other information needed to achieve high levels of sales.

Product guides are an essential part of the sales process and ensure that the salesforce have all the information needed to achieve high levels of market penetration. It is also important that the salesforce are aware of all the elements of the integrated marketing programme so that they can take full advantage of the opportunities. The communications programme would cover the following areas:

- Information on the advertising and direct marketing programmes that are currently operating.
- Advice on how to make the best use of the leads that are generated from the campaigns.
- Information on the consumer sales promotion and incentive programmes that are operating with full operational details so that they can explain them to customers and deal with any queries.
- Clear guidelines on the information that is needed to set up the customer database marketing operation. This ensures that the database can be used to complement future sales-force activity and the salesforce should be told how they will benefit from the information they are providing.
- Information on all the database marketing operations that are being carried out with their own customer base. This keeps the salesforce up-to-date with all the contact that is going on between them and ensures that there is no misunderstanding or duplication.

This communications package ensures that the salesforce play a role within the overall marketing programme and do not operate outside it. This is particularly appropriate if the company's organizational structure keeps sales and marketing activities in separate compartments. It is also essential when an organization such as an insurance company changes from selling individual products to marketing solutions and building long-term relationships with customers. The salesforce becomes part of the delivery mechanism for the solution and the direct sales activity must be fully integrated with the rest of the programme.

Distributor communications

The same principles of continuous communication can be applied to the agents and professional advisers who market the company's products. They may be tied agents or they may be independent advisers who recommend the appropriate product to their customers. The main communications tasks are similar to the salesforce tasks. However, there are a number of other important activities:

- Communications to persuade the independent advisers that the company's products are suitable – the distributor communications programme would be integrated with the direct marketing and campaigns that are running to recruit new distributors.
- Communications to support day-to-day operations between the company and its distributors. These would include administrative information on how to handle customer queries, policies and claims, methods of remuneration, reporting information, problem management procedures and other business processes. These are not part of a marketing campaign but they are important because they make it easy for the distributors to do business.
- Operating standards and customer focus standards that outline the company's policies for dealing with customers. This ensures that this company can offer a consistent national service to all customers through a diverse network. Consistency of service is integral to a successful relationship marketing programme. 'Performance scatter' can present customers with a bewildering variety of service standards from different outlets in the same way that a marketing programme which is not integrated can present different images to the customer. Consistent standards of customer service ensure that the integrated marketing programme is not damaged by poor performance at the point-of-sale.

- Guidelines on local marketing and business support. It is important to local business performance that distributors understand the level of support available to them and can make the best use of it. The guide would describe the support programmes and provide instructions on how to use it – how to run a direct marketing or local advertising programme for example, how to customize publications or create new publications within corporate guidelines. The communications programme ensures that marketing and support programmes are not wasted and that local outlets feel they are an integral part of the marketing process.

Retail Support

The insurance company used to illustrate this section would not have retail outlets, but this marketing process would be important to many companies. Retail outlets are the local point of contact with customers so it is essential that they have the facilities and the support to deliver a high standard of customer service. This support can take a number of forms:

- Providing product information and point-of-sale material for prospects and customers who visit the local branch
- Mailers or local advertisements that attract customers and prospects to the branch to meet consultants
- Corporate identity and display material that help to brand the outlet and provide a strong local presence
- Business and communications support to improve operational efficiency and standards of customer service. This might include information on training programmes, guidelines on standards of service and other support to improve operational efficiency
- Guidelines on delivering service
- Updates on product development and new marketing programmes.

Retail support activities should be fully integrated with other marketing activities so that the company can utilize the full potential of quality personal service through local outlets:

- Using direct marketing and local advertising to generate leads or store traffic for local outlets
- Providing database information to local outlets so that they can build relationships with local customers
- Using local public relations campaigns based around local community involvement and local activities

> - Running local events to attract prospects and customers
> - Cooperative programmes with local independent agents or advisers to ensure an integrated approach in the local market.

By strengthening relationships with local outlets, it is possible to extend the concept of personal service into the local market.

Product information

Product information is important to every type of business and it must be integrated with other communications elements. As part of the customer communications process, product information will be used extensively:

> - In response to requests generated via advertisements, direct marketing or enquiries from local advisers or local outlets
> - As part of a relationship marketing programme to keep customers up-to-date with commercial or product developments
> - As support material for the salesforce, local outlets or local advisers so that they can provide their customers with information.

Product information, in the form of brochures, leaflets, handbooks, information videos and other published material should reflect the overall corporate and communications objectives of the other elements of the marketing programme. Visual standards and key messages should be integrated so that the customer receives consistent messages in every form of communications. Publications should also be assigned specific tasks within the overall framework of the integrated marketing campaign.

It is easy to produce publications for their own sake – the 'we need a brochure' syndrome - regardless of a specific communications task. It is far better to assign publications a specific role, such as:

> - To provide a response mechanism to enquiries and give prospects sufficient information to make a decision about the product or service
> - To provide detailed information or personal illustration that cannot be communicated in a personal presentation
> - To provide information that is required by law.

In an integrated campaign, product information could have a number of roles and it is important that copy and design themes reflect the same messages and positioning statements.

Corporate identity

Corporate identity and corporate communications are an essential part of an integrated marketing campaign. They ensure that every form of communication is consistent and reinforces the customers' view of the company. An integrated marketing programme presents a consistent view of the company to the customer, and it is important that the visual identity reflects the company's planned position.

A corporate identity may not have been reviewed recently and may reflect older values. Insurance companies, for example, have traditionally utilized reassuring symbols as their logo, but these may not be in keeping with current values. Corporate identity influences every visual element of the company – publications, advertisements, correspondence, point-of-sale, direct mail.

Corporate communications should also be used to raise awareness of the company and explain its activities. The insurance company is managing its perceptions as a basis for future marketing programmes with a range of corporate communications activities:

- Corporate advertising in key consumer and professional media
- Corporate brochures explaining the company's position distributed to all or to selected customers
- Corporate messages in all direct marketing material
- Press information that describes recent corporate developments, in the form of feature articles, interviews or comment
- Corporate sponsorship of events that raise awareness among target groups.

Corporate communications should be used to reposition the company so that it reflects customer needs. Target perceptions would include:

- To be seen as a company that offers professional, impartial advice to customers and tailors solutions to the requirements of their lifestyle
- To be seen as a consultant that delivers whole-life solutions, rather than individual products
- To be seen as an innovative company that develops new solutions to meet customer needs.

Corporate communications like this can provide a good foundation for product communications.

Relationship marketing

Relationship marketing, like corporate communications, is a fundamental activity that supports all the other elements of an integrated campaign. Relationship marketing has customer retention as its main objective. It recognizes that it is more profitable to retain and grow business with existing customers than to keep on winning new clients. Retaining customers for life is the ultimate aim of relationship marketing programmes and it is a concept that is particularly important in the financial services sector.

Insurance companies recognize that it is particularly important in the financial services sector. Insurance companies recognize that their customer needs change through their lives and therefore it is important to retain constant contact. This means two major changes for the insurance company:

- Changing the role of the salesforce from new business getters to consultants who advise their customers on long-term planning
- Building and utilizing a database to ensure that a targeted approach can be made to each customer.

Relationship marketing is based on regular, quality customer contact with information that reflects customers' needs. Relationship marketing begins when the company establishes contact with the new customer and it is integrated with the other campaign elements:

- Lead generation programmes utilizing advertisements and direct marketing are designed to provide information for the database.
- Follow-up direct marketing and telemarketing utilizes information from the initial enquiry to provide the customer with targeted communications and offers.
- Promotional and incentive activities are targeted to customers' needs, and the current stage of account development. Incentives can be used to encourage commitment to first purchase, trade-up to a higher value policy or to cross-sell other products in the range.
- Planned direct marketing and telemarketing can be utilized at regular intervals to ensure regular contact with customers to keep them informed or to arrange appointments with consultants.
- Salesforce and distributor programmes can be integrated with the relationship marketing programme to ensure that sales staff concentrate on building relationships rather than short-term sales.

Summary

This chapter outlines the key elements or 'building blocks' of an integrated marketing campaign. It shows how the advertising, direct marketing, telemarketing, press information, internal communications, sales promotion and incentives, salesforce communications, distributor communications, retail support, product and technical information, corporate identity and corporate communications, and relationship marketing can be used to complement each other and strengthen the overall impact of a campaign.

3 Approaches to planning

Introduction

This chapter describes the process of planning an integrated campaign. It shows how the planning process varies from conventional campaign planning and can be used as the basis for developing individual plans.

Setting overall objectives

Like most business plans, the integrated marketing plan begins with an overview of the activity. This is developed from corporate objectives and can take a number of forms:

> ● To improve return on investment and improve profitability
> ● To establish market leadership in current markets
> ● Develop a strong presence in new markets
> ● Rationalize the company's product range and operations to compete effectively.

These overall objectives form part of any marketing plan, but in an integrated marketing structure they are even more important because they affect the direction the company marketing is taking. In formulating these overall objectives, you should include background information on current marketing and financial performance, competitive performance, market conditions and prospects, key influencing factors and your planned position. A statement of direction will help to put current and future marketing activities into context and will provide an overall framework which enables the individual marketing elements to be related to each other. The important questions are:

> ● What is your overall objective for the current year and the long term?
> ● How does this translate into financial objectives and market share objectives?
> ● How does this compare with current and historical performance?
> ● How does this translate into financial objectives and market share objectives?
> ● How does this compare with current and historical performance?

Marketing objectives

The overall objectives need to be translated into marketing objectives. Comprehensive self-assessment is a useful starting point:

- What are the key market sectors for development?
- Are these new sectors or does the company already have a presence?
- What is the company's performance in each sector and how does it compare with competitive performance?
- What competitive activities will influence opportunities in each of the company's sectors?
- What action will the company take to counter these competitive actions?
- What marketing resources are currently under-utilized and how successfully are they performing?
- What level of resource is currently available and how could it be improved?
- What are the sales objectives and how are they broken down by sector and by key account?
- What is the ratio of business between direct sales and sales through retail outlets and distributors?
- What is the split between sales to existing customers and new customers?
- Who are the key accounts in the customer base?
- What is the current level of marketing support activities and how effectively is it being used?
- How would marketing support be measured and what would be the key indicators of successful performance?
- How is the salesforce structured and how does this relate to the overall marketing objectives?
- How is salesforce performance measured and can it be measured in relation to support levels?
- Does the current distributor network work effectively?
- How is direct marketing used and is it integrated with other activities such as direct response advertising, telemarketing, exhibitions and sales support?
- How well are local outlets supported and what form does the support take?
- Can local marketing performance be measured?
- Would it be more beneficial to develop customized local marketing material or to operate standard national programmes?

- Are your local outlets offering a consistent standard of service to customers or are there variations that influence overall customer satisfaction?
- What form of support would achieve the necessary consistency and help local outlets to improve their business performance?
- How does the direct salesforce fit into the overall marketing programme and how is it supported in terms of presentation material, advertising back up, incentive programmes, product and skills training?
- Could other elements of the marketing mix be used to improve salesforce performance?
- How successfully do the salesforce operate key account management and could they benefit from integrated marketing?
- Will overall growth come from new business or the development of existing accounts?
- What measures will be needed to ensure success in each of these activities?
- Does your product range match the requirements of the marketplace and what plans do you have to rationalize or extend the range?
- Will the changes in the range require new product launches or could they be handled through consistent product information programmes?
- What type of product information will be more appropriate?
- Does it need detailed product information and would personal demonstration be important?
- How important will exhibitions and seminars be in launching the product?
- If the product is conceptual or innovative, what level of marketing support will be required to ensure awareness and acceptance?
- Will the company be entering new markets or new territories?
- What marketing actions will be needed to succeed in these territories?
- Can the company succeed through direct or indirect sales methods?
- What form and level of support will be needed to succeed in these markets?
- Is the company changing its main activities or will there be a focus on customer care?
- What level of internal communications will be needed to achieve high levels of understanding and awareness?
- How crucial is corporate commitment to overall success?

- If the company is undertaking a new corporate identity or getting involved in mergers or takeovers, what impact will this have on the company's overall success?
- How well are these changes understood and what actions should be taken to increase awareness?

By carrying out this kind of detailed self-assessment, it is possible to arrive at the key marketing objectives. In an integrated marketing programme it is important to take a broad view because so many elements are interacting rather than operating in isolation. The marketing analysis requires a 'what if' approach – what if we introduced telemarketing, what if we redeployed the salesforce and made greater use of direct marketing, what if we dropped our advertising budget and improved the standard of technical communications?

Planning an integrated marketing campaign requires this additional element of comparison to determine the best option from many different choices.

Audit and research

The previous section listed many different questions that should be asked before setting marketing objectives. Many of the topics should be assessed by independent audit and research to determine the key marketing and communications tasks. Research should be carried out internally and externally because attitudes are important in both areas.

An initial audit is carried out to undertake levels of awareness and understanding of the company and its products and to see whether the current communications programmes reflect the integrated marketing objectives. The company is trying to find out whether its key customer-facing staff understand the company's current direction. The company also audits its current marketing publications to see whether they reflect the current position. The audit could be extended to see whether the company's current communications programmes are working in an integrated way. The audit could be at the creative/visual level:

- Do the communications all reflect consistent visual standards?
- Do they incorporate consistent messages?
- Are there important distinctions between different products and services and divisions?
- Can they be rationalized to strengthen the overall corporate image and will this activity benefit the consumer?
- How is the company actually providing its marketing communications material and is this making integration difficult?

The audit of internal communications can be supplemented by external research into perceptions of the company:

- Is the company seen as a leader in its field?
- What do buyers think are its main products?
- What do buyers see as the main benefits of the company and its products and services?
- What are the perceptions of competitors and their key strengths?
- What improvements would buyers like to see in product or service performance?
- What are the key criteria for selecting product and supplier?
- Who is involved in the decision-making process and what are their most important concerns?
- What would the buyers be looking for in selecting new suppliers?
- How does the buyer rate suppliers and is there any formal system for evaluating suppliers?

The most important part of the research programme is how buyers get their information and what sort of information they need. By focusing on this aspect of the buying process, the integrated marketing plan will take account of all the decision-making factors and be aimed precisely at the target audience.

Conventional research also yields valuable information for developing product benefits and creative strategies and it is essential that full research is available to the agency team.

Concerns of the target audience

An effective communications programme tells buyers what they need to know, not what a supplier wants them to know. An integrated marketing programme should help decision makers make informed decisions. If the information does not answer their questions or provide a basis for selecting then the information is wasted.

These concerns vary by different members of the target audience and it is important to distinguish them in carrying out research.

A senior management team would be concerned about the overall impact of a product or service on their organization – will it help them to improve competitive performance or overcome operational problems? For example, a new product that allows a customer to enter new markets or achieve market leadership will be a strategically important product and that becomes a major concern for the decision-making team.

Functional directors will be responsible for the performance of specific activities and they will be interested in detailed assessment of the benefits of the product. Their concerns will be product benefit, value for money and contribution to the success of their operations.

Technical specialists want to know about the technical performance of the product. How can it help the customer to get improved performance from their own products and if they are going to change what is the risk factor involved and how can the company minimize this. Technical specialists want to know that new technology is proven. Innovation is interesting but if it is not commercially proven it may not be of real interest to technical people.

Purchasing departments are concerned with value for money and with improving the overall quality of their service to internal departments. They make an increasing contribution to total quality and they need to know how their product or service will change that. At a more basic level they are concerned with the commercial aspects of the relationship – can the supplier sustain the standards of delivery and service that are needed, what corporate developments will help to improve standards of service and does the company have the long-term financial stability to remain a competitive and reliable supplier? Overall the purchasing team want to know that it will be easy to do business with the company.

This set of concerns is more appropriate to the business-to-business sector but similar concerns can be applied to the consumer sector. Research can be used to extract key reasons to buy and these should be developed into an overall picture of the consumer.

Planned perceptions

The information that is derived from research and analysis of the target audience can be used to develop a set of target perceptions for the company. Planned perceptions represent the way you want to be seen by customers and prospects. These perceptions could include:

- The leading player in the market
- A successful global player
- A company dedicated to customer service
- An innovative company committed to leading edge solutions
- An easy company to do business with
- A company conveniently located for nationwide service
- A company supplying the widest range of services and products
- A lifetime of service
- Covering your changing needs.

Research and audits will indicate how far or how near you are to achieving target perceptions and you can use the 'perception gap' to develop a set of positioning messages that should be built into every aspect of integrated marketing. Planned perceptions should be measured. A company that knew it had only achieved its planned perception with 25 per cent of the target audience could measure progress at the end of a campaign or a budget period. By varying the elements of the marketing and communications programme it could determine the strategy that had the greatest impact.

Integrated communications objectives

Integrated communications objectives are determined by research and the planned perceptions programme. A broad communications objective might be to raise awareness of the company's products and resources among all potential prospects and customers or to convince potential distributors that the company's franchise is valuable. The objective can then be made more specific, for example convincing a group of regional distributors that participation in a specific incentive programme will help them to increase sales of a product range. Another specific objective might be to convince four key buyers that they should specify the company's products.

Media selection

An integrated marketing solution uses the most appropriate media and techniques to achieve marketing objectives. There is no 'lead' technique and the solution could include any of the following:

- Advertising
- Direct marketing
- Telemarketing
- Public relations
- Internal communications
- Incentives
- Salesforce communications
- Distributor communications
- Retail support
- Product and technical information
- Corporate identity and corporate communications
- Presentations and exhibitions
- Relationship marketing.

While conventional media planning techniques concentrate on buying advertising space effectively, integrated marketing takes a more fundamental look at the whole range of media available. Which of the media are most appropriate for the integrated marketing task? Which media should be incorporated to support other activitie?.

Chapter 2 used the example of the insurance company to illustrate how the different 'building blocks' work together. In a campaign like that, the three leading media are likely to be advertising, direct marketing and telemarketing. Research shows that, when they are used together in an integrated campaign, they can achieve high response and conversion rates.

However, this may not be the most appropriate combination for other product or market sectors. The exercises in Chapter 10 can provide useful guidelines on developing a plan for different sectors.

Summary

Planning an integrated marketing communications programme differs from conventional campaign planning. The process of self-assessment is important to identify the priorities in the planning process. Self-assessment should be reinforced by independent audit and research to establish the key tasks for the programme. Planned perceptions are a valuable basis for developing creative strategies and measuring the overall effectiveness of the campaign.

4 Scenarios for integrated marketing

Introduction

This chapter looks at ways in which you can decide whether integrated marketing is appropriate for your business. Although the benefits of integrated marketing appear to be universal, there are scenarios which make it more suitable:

- Your company faces complex issues in the marketplace or your products raise complex issues within the customer company.
- To market your products or services effectively, you must convince many different decision makers. Your communications programme must work consistently across all decision makers.
- You are involved in market development projects and it is essential that you carry out market education as well as developing sales.
- You operate through multiple sales channels and it is essential that each one of these operates effectively.
- You are introducing new product programmes and you need to convince different groups of people that your products will benefit that organization.
- Research shows that important decision makers and influencers hold poor perceptions of your organization and it is vital that you reposition the organization.
- Limited budgets mean that every element of the programme must work harder and some of the media represent better value for money.
- You are operating in niche markets and you need to ensure that your marketing performance is consistent across all sectors.
- Your company is undergoing significant change and you need to ensure that messages are communicated consistently to every member of the target audience.
- You are introducing a local marketing strategy and you wish to ensure that you offer consistent levels of service and support throughout a network.

These scenarios are explained in more detail in the remainder of this chapter and the techniques for operating the programmes are described in other chapters including Chapter 5 'Suporting business objectives'. To help you relate the scenarios to your own business, each one includes a checklist of warning signs.

Complex issues

As consultants Arthur Andersen explained in a recruitment advertisement, 'It is no easier to communicate change than it is to implement it.' Behind this statement was a belief that change is only successful if everyone in an organization understands the reasons for change and is aware of their role. Change is one complex issue and other activities such as the introduction of technology or the development of new working practices have an equal complexity, Andersen's solution was to recruit people who understood the process of integrated marketing so that they could communicate effectively at every level and ensure that everyone in the organization was able to take the appropriate action.

Internal awareness

Complexity is a relative term and it is essential that the organization understands the different levels of awareness.

- What key issues are you or your clients facing – new technology, changes in the marketplace, launch of new products, organizational structure, mergers or acquisitions, new legislation?
- What impact will these issues have on your organization.
- What is the current level of understanding?
- Who needs to understand the changes and what perception should they hold?
- What are the key communications channels to these target groups?
- Can you audit the internal communications processes?
- Are each of the target groups receiving the same messages?
- How could the messages be presented more consistently?
- What media are used to communicate and how could these media be used more cost effectively?
- How can the performance of the communications programme be measured?

These questions will help you analyse the internal communications process that is used to get across these complex issues. Integrated marketing will ensure that you focus on the most important issues and utilize appropriate media to achieve full understanding.

External awareness

Complex issues raised by your products or services may also have an impact on your clients or other groups. If we take the example of an innovative new product, this could have a far-reaching impact on your clients' business:

- Will your products have an impact on your clients' working practices?
- Will your products change the shape of their technology?
- Will it require change in their design or manufacturing processes?
- Could your product or service give your clients a greater competitive edge?
- What changes would they need to make to take advantage of their competitive position and the introduction of your product or service?
- Who are the key influencers and decision makers within the customer organization?
- What information do they need to make positive decisions?
- How can you help them to improve their decision-making process?
- What information would be needed to ensure the correct level of decision making?

An integrated marketing programme will ensure that all of these issues are dealt with systematically and that each of the decision processes is handled efficiently. Other groups outside your own or your customers' organizations may be important to your overall development strategy:

- Is it essential that the media, politicians or other groups of influencers understand the issues?
- What is their current level of understanding?
- What are the communications channels for reaching the important groups?
- Can the channels reach the target audience efficiently?

Effectiveness of the media

The other consideration is whether the media are able to handle the messages effectively:

- Do your current communications channels allow you to communicate complex issues?
- If you are using advertisements or video are your audiences able to grasp the main issues within the timespan of the medium?
- Could publications or management guides help to communicate even greater levels of detail and improve understanding?
- Would photographs, case histories or other forms of illustration help to clarify complex issues?
- Do generic issues need to be personalized and communicated through direct channels to improve perception and understanding?
- Would permanent reference media be more valuable in building long-term understanding?

As we said at the beginning of this section, complexity is a relative issue. While a senior management team may have an immediate grasp of an issue, middle managers or employees who are affected by the issue may find it more difficult to grasp. The scenario must take account of the audience's understanding as well as the qualities of the medium.

Large decision-making groups

Integrated marketing is vital if you have to convince a large number of different decision makers or if the decision-making process is complex. In business-to-business markets this is generally the norm and complexity varies with the level of risk of the product. Standard purchasing scenarios can help to quantify the levels of risk.

Routine purchasing scenarios

The routine repurchase involves the lowest level of risk: A customer continues to buy the same product from the same supplier. Provided the supplier is able to maintain consistency of quality, delivery and price, there is minimal risk and the communications needs are minimal.

Add a new competitor to the scenario and the purchase department has to make a different set of decisions. They might be offered better quality, lower prices, improved delivery or a different specification. The current supplier must convince the customer that the present service is sufficient or offer improvements. The communications requirements are still simple – to reinforce the relationship with the purchasing department or to introduce a new offer. If the change involves a considerable degree of change then the purchasing scenario is now different – it is a modified repurchase and this requires a different communications strategy.

Changing the specification

The specification has changed. The purchasing department is no longer buying the same product. The new specification could have an impact on the customers' products in terms of its performance and manufacturing complexity. The onus is on the supplier to communicate that change. The internal communications programme should now include communications aimed at the technical department and the manufacturing manager. If they accept the benefits of the new specification the purchasing department can continue to order in the same way.

A new supplier

If the purchasing department decides to use a new supplier, the process can become more complex. The new supplier has to demonstrate that these alternative products or services meet design, technical and manufacturing requirements. As well as any communications aimed at the manufacturing or technical departments, the new supplier must also demonstrate supplier capability. If the product or service is strategically important, decisions about changes of supplier may be referred to the senior management team. Is the company convinced that the new supplier can meet quality, delivery and technical requirements consistently over the long term? What is the suppliers reputation and track record in the market? What capability and resources does the new supplier bring to bear and how do these compare with existing suppliers?

A new specification and a new supplier

So far the scenarios have concentrated on the repurchase of an existing product. If a company launches a new product the process becomes more complex. The new product may offer the customer key competitive advantages but these have to be carefully evaluated before proceeding. A new material used in aerospace to produce lightweight strong components is marketed to the engineering sector. It promises benefits of weight reduction, strength, design flexibility, manufacturing ability and reduction of through-life costs because of reduced maintenance and improved performance. Overall, the product offers the customer the opportunity to market a range of higher specification and therefore improve its competitiveness. However, the product costs more than conventional materials.

The decision-making process will now include a much wider group of people and it is vital that the decision-making process covers them all. The senior management team must understand the strategic benefits of the new product – how will it help them to improve market penetration by offering higher performance products? The technical department need to understand the performance levels of the new product and learn new design techniques so that they can make the most of its new properties. Their communications programmes must include performance data, application information and design guidelines so that they learn to use the new product rather than reject it as being unfamiliar.

The marketing department will have responsibility for marketing a product range that incorporates new benefits. The communications programme explains how this can improve their performance over competitive offerings and will help them to identify sector opportunities. Manufacturing could be a major stumbling block to acceptance of the product; this could outweigh any marketing advantages and create opportunities within the company. The integrated marketing programme therefore needs to deal with potential opportunities within the customer company as well as attracting high levels of support from the group who stand to benefit most from the changes.

The finance department, for example, may decide that the increase in costs is not justified. However, this may reflect their lack of understanding of the overall benefits of the programme. The product offers increased marketing performance, lower through-life costs and therefore reduced expenditure on system support and maintenance. Customer dissatisfaction will be reduced, cutting the cost of customer retention. Any investment in new manufacturing technology will be counterbalanced by greater market performance and long-term profit.

The decision-making process operates at many different levels and will progress through a number of different stages. The integrated marketing programme must take account of all the different concerns and interests and must therefore utilize broadcast and targeted media. A communications grid can form an important part of the communications planning process when dealing with complex decision-making scenarios.

Market development

Market development, like the communication of complex issues and the management of large decision-making groups, requires a wide-ranging marketing and communications strategy which could use external as well as corporate communications resources:

- How well does the market understand the benefits and features of the product?
- Would greater understanding improve the opportunities for market penetration?
- How could external influencers affect likely market success?
- How do people get information that will improve their understanding of products and services?

Market development can occur in a number of different situations:

- A company is introducing new technology that has not been tried before
- The company is attempting to transfer technology from another application area and needs to build understanding in the new sector
- The company is planning joint developments with customers or other manufacturers and wants to convince partners that the new move will be of mutual benefit.

The process of communications is similar to the complex decision-making process where it is vital to integrate communications to the different groups of people who might benefit. The process is top-down:

- Will the change have strategic benefit? If so, does the communications programme include elements that are targeted at executive decision makers?
- What information can be provided to the senior decision - making team that will enable them to cascade the information down the organization?
- Should the information come from an independent/external source such as a consultant? What are the communications channels for reaching the independent influencers and what form of support will help them to get the message across effectively?

It is not always a strategic task and the drive may come from decision makers lower down in the organization. If they are convinced that the new product or service will provide major corporate benefits, they need the support to present the case within their own organization. The introduction of just-in-time (JIT) technology, for example, involved efforts both by industry groups such as the Department of Trade and Industry and manufacturing groups who would support JIT, such as computer and communications systems suppliers. Manufacturing consultants who would be responsible for introducing the new techniques into their own organization felt it was important that management understood the full implications if the changes JIT would bring. The marketing development programme was therefore a joint development between at least three different groups and integrated marketing would have ensured that messages were presented consistently. It is too easy in a new product launch to assume that customers will rush to buy a new product simply because of inherent benefits. If a prospect does not understand how the product or service is to be used, marketing communications will be wasted. An integrated marketing programme will therefore concentrate on raising awareness and understanding across the target market.

Multiple sales channels

Advertising and other forms of communication can be used to stimulate demand for a product, but if the prospect does not know where to buy the product, the consumer advertising could be wasted. A consumer product for example could be available through mail order, from selected retail outlets, direct from the manufacturer via off the page direct response advertising, through authorized distributors or from a direct salesforce. Before allocating marketing expenditure, it is essential to evaluate which of the sales channels is likely to be the most productive:

- Does direct mail provide you with access to a large proportion of the target market?
- Do the media provide prospects with sufficient buying information to make a purchasing decision?
- Do retail outlets carry your product exclusively or do they also offer competitive products? How well do retail staff understand products, customers, benefits and the marketplace?
- Does the retail outlet provide a suitable environment for marketing the product? Does it provide suitable coverage of the market? Will the prospects get enough information from the advertisements to make a purchasing decision?
- Direct response advertising can represent a cost-effective method of marketing the product. Does it provide suitable coverage of the market? Will the prospects get enough information from advertising to make a purchasing decision?
- Authorized distributors, like retail outlets, have to be developed to market the product successfully and the communications programme will be similar.
- The direct salesforce may be appropriate in certain circumstances but it also needs to be developed and supported through marketing communications to ensure that it operates effectively. Does your salesforce communications programme enable you to keep the salesforce up-to-date with the latest product developments? Is there a sales incentive structure which will focus the effort on the right product group? Do direct marketing and advertising programmes help to generate sufficient leads for the salesforce? Does a database marketing programme help to build up long-term relationships with customers ?

Poor perceptions

Does your company suffer from poor perceptions by customers, employees or investors? If so, it can have a negative effect on your business performance and prevent you from achieving your marketing objectives. If research shows that your competitors are better regarded in areas where you know you are stronger, your customers' views may need to be changed. A managed perception programme helps to ensure that your customers and other important groups share your target perceptions. An integrated communications programme is an essential part of the management process:

- What is your target perception in terms of market leadership or effective business performance?
- Have you carried out research into target perceptions?
- Who are the key influencers in the decision-making process?
- What factors do they consider important?
- What is the gap between target perception and the actual perception identified by research?
- What are the key messages that need to be communicated to each group?
- How do the target audience currently receive information?
- How complex is the information they need to receive and what are the most suitable media for communication?

Perception management becomes a key issue in a number of different scenarios:

- When a company is undergoing significant change and image is crucial to the achievement of new contracts
- When share price or investor confidence is low
- When the company is seeking to expand its operations or move into new markets.

Perception management is a crucial part of strategic business development and it should therefore be high on the agenda of the senior management team. It differs from traditional corporate financial communications and should be integrated with all other forms of communication. The factors influencing a company's perception include its current product range, market performance, reputation in the industry, development plans and statement of direction, recruitment and training policies, quality of staff, customer relations and customer satisfaction levels. Financial performance, investment levels and other corporate initiatives also influence perception so communications about any of those areas should be incorporated in a perception management programme.

Perception management can also be integrated with a new corporate identity programme. The identity programme provides visible evidence of the company's position and this is reinforced by a programme of planned perceptions. For example, an identity programme that presented the image of a dynamic organization with a reputation for innovation should be strengthened by communications that give examples of innovation and are targeted at the right decision makers. If your organization has recently carried out an overhaul of the corporate identity, look closely at current perceptions of your company:

- Who are the key people who need to be influenced?
- How does the visual identity compare with the overall perception?
- Is there a conflict between the corporate identity and the image of any division or operating unit? Divisions who run their own communications programmes are tightly focused on their own specific market sectors but it is important that they contribute to overall corporate image.

Limited budget

Integrated marketing is a cost-effective solution for companies with budget limitations. An organization with a small budget could waste its funds with expenditure on advertising because reach and frequency may not be sufficient to deliver effective penetration of the market. The problem becomes worse when a company with a limited budget is trying to reach a diverse marketplace with different types of prospects, all having different communications requirements.

An integrated communications programme on the other hand utilizes media that are tightly focused on the target market and selects those that deliver the message in the most cost-effective way.

A franchised car dealer, for example running a parts and service operation might consider that advertising in the local press could be the most effective solution for reaching the target market, which is motorists and the trade. However, closer evaluation shows that a higher percentage of business communications comes from trade sales to parts retailers, fleet operators, wholesalers, independent service operators and other car dealers who require both parts and service. Direct marketing to the main customers in each group is identified as the most effective method of improving market penetration and increasing customer loyalty. The dealer finds that writing to customers each month with information on different aspects of the dealership service builds greater awareness and understanding than occasional advertising in local papers.

The regular high level of communications also helps to build important communications between customers and dealership and demonstrates that the relationship can be mutually beneficial. It is more important to achieve measurable results with a limited budget. A campaign should not simply be run for the sake of it: it should be run to achieve a specific objective – to raise awareness by x per cent, to generate y enquiries, to deliver key messages to z prospects. If a single medium like direct marketing cannot deliver the whole result it is essential to back it with techniques such as telemarketing which reinforce the impact of the campaign and help to deliver results.

Although budget limitations can lead to individual one-off programmes, integrated marketing will help to strengthen overall impact. A consistent creative theme or the reinforcement of a continuous campaign will help to ensure that prospects and customers are aware of the overall corporate strengths.

Niche market programmes

When a company moves into other markets, it needs to be able to use its overall corporate strengths in the new markets. Transferred values are only possible when communications are totally integrated and when the corporate values can be transferred into other sectors.

For example, a computer manufacturer who has a successful track record in marketing to the government sector identifies opportunities in the manufacturing sector. The sector demands not just good IT supply, but also consultancy, project management, training and management services. Although the computer manufacturer does not have a track record in these new sectors, it identifies that the total solution of products and services will be a vital element in determining overall success.

An integrated campaign would not focus on negative points – the company's limited experience in the manufacturing sector – but would stress its overall capability in the key areas of IT development showing how its total solution strategy has helped equipment manufacturers achieve corporate success. The campaign would not alter significantly from sector to sector and would include positioning messages that are relevant to all sectors.

The umbrella programme can easily be customized by incorporating specific elements of direct marketing that are applied to each sector. For example, publications and management guides can be easily tailored to the needs of individual market sectors while presentations and other documentation can be tailored at the same level. A programme which succeeds in one sector may not easily transfer to other areas, but it builds corporate strengths and helps to reinforce them.

The corporate publications and other corporate communications can also utilize the individual sector messages to present overall corporate capability. This makes it easier for companies to develop future strategies and to prepare the ground for specific sector communications. In planning niche marketing communications, it is important to distinguish between corporate and niche marketing activities. Corporate activities such as advertising, capability brochures and presentations, corporate public relations and product information can be produced centrally to provide coverage of all sectors in a cost-effective way, while direct marketing and targeted sectors precisely convey the specific messages to each individual sector.

Niche marketing does not need niche communications techniques but simply the customization of different elements of the marketing mix.

Local market development

Local marketing is a neglected area – companies who market their products or services through local outlets depend on effective local marketing. However, unless the local outlets are strictly controlled and operate according to competitive guidelines, local marketing performance will be, at least, fragmented and may be extremely weak:

- Are your local outlets franchised or under your direct control?
- Do you have written agreements conveying local marketing activities?
- Can you implement consistent standards in each of your local branches?
- Is each branch free to operate its own individual marketing programmes?
- How do you coordinate local marketing activities?
- Can you provide local marketing support material suitable for consistent presentation of a corporate image or is material supplied on an ad hoc basis for independent local marketing activities?
- Do you want to brand your local outlets so that you can promote them as a group rather than a series of individual outlets?
- Do your customers make use of multiple branches or do branch differences not matter?
- What are the key customer and operating standards that can be applied to the whole branch network?
- How could an integrated communications programme help to reinforce the process?

An integrated local marketing programme is dependent on the application of consistent performance standards and the need for a nationally branded product. Traditional local support programmes have taken the form of a crude support advertisement or direct marketing programme which stresses the benefits of using that branch and attempts to present a consistent picture of national service.

An integrated campaign provides the opportunity to build up a picture of a powerful local network which can be treated as a single brand. This type of umbrella campaign is far stronger than a series of ad hoc local campaigns and strengthens the impact of targeted local marketing: 'Trust an *** outlet to provide you with superb standards of service'. The theme can then be repeated at local level and the local outlet can supplement it with special products and services which reflect local market conditions.

Do your local outlets believe they are part of a national team or do they feel isolated? Communications programmes which keep members of a dealer network up-to-date with developments in the rest of the network can help to build a sense of team spirit and ensure that benefits are transferred from one branch to another. Competition between branches can also play a role in improving standards. For example, sales incentive or customer satisfaction programmes in which branches compete against each other in leagues helps to improve overall standards and ensures that local marketing is not operated in isolation. A local marketing programme should therefore concentrate on the needs of local customers but reflect the strength of the overall organization.

Summary

Integrated marketing may not be appropriate for every organization. However, there are a number of important factors that help to indicate the need for integrated marketing:

Your company faces complex issues in the marketplace or your products raise complex issues within the customer company.

To market your products or services effectively, you must convince many different decision makers and your communications programme must work consistently across all decision makers.

You are involved in market development projects and it is essential that you carry out market education as well as developing sales.

You operate through multiple sales channels and it essential that each one of these operates effectively.

You are introducing new product programmes and you need to convince different groups of people that your products will benefit that organization.

Research shows that important decision makers and influencers hold poor perceptions of your organization and it is vital that you reposition the organization.

Limited budgets mean that every element of the programme must work harder and some of the media represent better value for money.

You are operating in niche markets and you need to ensure that your marketing performance is consistent across all sectors.

Your company is undergoing significant change and you need to ensure that messages are communicated consistently to every member of the target audience.

You are introducing a local marketing strategy and you wish to ensure that you offer consistent levels of service and support throughout a network.

If any of these factors apply you should seriously consider integrated marketing.

5 Supporting business objectives

Introduction

Integrated marketing is most effective when it is used to support strategic business objectives. It is not just a tool for improving the results of an advertising campaign or making better use of below-the-line budgets. Integrated marketing can be used to achieve strategic objectives such as:

- Improved sales performance
- Building partnership
- Achieving customer focus
- Managing change
- Improving local marketing performance
- Providing effective product support
- Communicating quality.

A company might face some or all of these issues, but in each case they must ensure that they integrate all forms of communication.

Improving sales performance

In many sectors, salesforce performance is key to the success of the overall marketing strategy. In the capital goods sector, for example, personal contact at many different levels is vital to the successful negotiation of a major system or product contract. Although the salesforce take the lead in the marketing operation, it is essential that the other elements of the marketing programme are integrated in a way that provides maximum support for the salesforce. These are some of the key actions that can be taken:

- Running direct response advertisements in purchasing and technical journals inviting readers to request free consultation or information packs. This will provide the salesforce with valuable leads to follow up and will also give prospects useful background information which will make the salesforce's introductory meetings more useful. The response could highlight decision makers who may not be known to the marketing team.

- Running advertisements in purchasing and technical journals which describe the consultation and advisory services available from the salesforce. An informative advertisement like this helps to build customer confidence in the salesforce and a belief that a sales meeting could be mutually beneficial.
- Press support in purchasing and technical journals using case histories of successful technical support to demonstrate the contribution the salesforce can make. Editorial coverage reinforces the press advertisements and allows the company to communicate more detailed information on salesforce capability.

The first three activities help to generate leads for the salesforce and provide introductory information to the prospect which makes the presentation easier.

- Telemarketing can be used to follow up the enquiries generated through advertising and public relations activities by qualifying the enquiries and making appointments for the salesforce to make personal visits.

The next series of activities is designed to reinforce personal sales skills and ensure that each call is highly productive

- Product and technical information is produced which reflects the visual standards and creative themes of the advertising campaigns and provides each decision maker with comprehensive information.
- The literature programme is structured to reflect the different concerns and information needs of each member of the decision-making team. This ensures that the decision-making team is fully informed and receptive to the salesforce presentation.
- Presentation support material to ensure that the salesforce can present consistently and professionally to the client. This could take the form of slide-tape, video or OHP presentations, or presentation binders with supporting documentation.

To reinforce the presentation and personal sales activities, direct marketing can be used to follow up and build relationships with key contacts as the decision-making process moves through its important stages. This relationship marketing programme will complement the programme of direct sales calls and reach contacts who may not be accessible to the salesforce.

- Targeted technical communications including proposals which are developed specifically for individual customers.
- Technical updates on projects or products which are relevant to the project under review.
- Corporate communications aimed at the senior management group within the decision-making team. This might include copies of capability brochures specially developed for the client.
- Special offers of business information or business services to support the main purchase. These might include reprints of papers or invitations to seminars on relevant industry topics. These activities help to reinforce the concepts presented in advertising and public relations of the salesforce as a valuable form of support and advice.

These activities help the salesforce to build strong relationships through a complex decision-making process, but what of the salesforce themselves? An integrated campaign should also reflect their specific requirements:

- Salesforce communications should be used to keep the salesforce up-to-date with business and technical developments within the organization. This ensures that they are fully informed on all aspects of the business and have all the information they need to present a complete picture of the company and deal with any questions.
- Product and marketing material. To ensure that members of the sales team are fully familiar with every aspect of the product they are selling, training material needs to be integrated with the rest of the programme. Ideally, the programme should focus on specific client information as well as general product information so that the salesforce are working to a tightly defined plan.

This integrated support programme helps to make the most of direct sales resources. Although the salesforce take the initiative and drive the programme, they are not acting in isolation. The integrated marketing programme keeps their clients informed and helps them to develop high levels of contact at every stage of the purchase process.

Building partnership

Building partnership with key accounts is an integral part of long-term marketing strategy. In partnership, two companies working together to achieve material business benefits drive down costs and get products to market quicker. Partnership communications are therefore important to building understanding and the right sort of relationship. There are three main stages in partnership communications:

- Presenting partnership communications
- Introducing the concept of partnership
- Presenting partnership capability.

Integration is vital at every stage because many different parties are involved on both sides and it is essential that everyone operates on common ground.

Partnership with important customers can be crucial to long-term business success. This section explains how you can introduce the concept of partnership to your key customers. You have identified the important partnership opportunities and you understand why partnership will benefit your customers. Before you can build a partnership relationship, you need to convince your customers that they should review the potential benefits of partnership within their organization and you may need to help them do that. There are three important stages:

- Introducing the concept of partnership at a strategic level
- Helping customers evaluate the benefits of partnership
- Putting together a partnership proposal.

Continuous, targeted and integrated communications are important at each stage and this section explains some of the techniques that can be used to present the case for partnership.

Introducing the concept of partnership

Adopting partnership is a strategic issue, not a purchasing problem. It is therefore essential that partnership is discussed at board level, because without commitment from the top your customers are unlikely to make the fundamental business changes that will enable them to benefit from partnership. Senior executives, however, may not be familiar with your company, or your products and services, and they may not understand why your products or services are strategically important to their business.

When ICL Customer Service Division wanted to build partnership with their important customers, they had to completely reposition customer services from an unavoidable cost element to an integral element of the competitive edge. Previous communications had concentrated on purchasing executives and the information systems managers responsible for support service. These were not the people who would make the decisions about partnership. They targeted communications at key decision makers which explained how partnership services could help them concentrate on their core business by making the most of their internal skills and resources. The communications programme concentrated on the customer's own business issues and used scenarios to explain how services could improve business performance. ICL took every opportunity to communicate these messages to business leaders at industry conferences and seminars, executive briefings and customer user-groups meetings. The face-to-face programme was backed by management reports, and feature articles in influential management publications.

The ICL programme shows that ad hoc communications are unlikely to achieve a change in perception. Positioning a company as a potential partner requires sustained communications over a period of time.

Reaching all the decision makers

There are a number of important members of a customer partnership team. Each of them will contribute in different ways to the decision to set up a partnership, but you must ensure that your integrated communications programme reaches each of them effectively:

- Senior executives are a prime contact in the initial stages when you are trying to raise awareness of the strategic benefits of partnership. Your task is to convince them that partnership will help them improve their business performance. The intended perception is that partnership is an integral part of building and maintaining the competitive edge. As a result of your communications programme, senior executives should set up a task force to further investigate the feasibility of partnership.
- Departmental managers may be involved in the initial stages as initiators of the need for partnership. By explaining, through communications, how partnership could help to improve the performance of their department, you may be able to create demand for partnership within the organization. As a result of your communications programme, departmental managers should present a case to their executive team for investigating potential partnership benefits.

- Purchasing executives are likely to be involved in the initial stages because of the major change in the relationship between supplier and customer. Your task is to explain how partnership will provide added-value solutions which ensure business benefits beyond the cost of the product or service. As a result of your communications programme, purchasing executives should open discussions with you and within their own organizations on the feasibility of partnership.

Using seminars to build partnership

In deciding what form the seminar should take, you should consider:

- Will the audience include the types of company and the target audience you want to reach? If you are inviting delegates, you decide the audience, but if the seminar is open, you need to know who the organizers are targeting.
- Does the seminar have a theme and programme that corresponds with the values of your partnership programme? For example, an open seminar on 'Manufacturing in the 1990s' would be appropriate for an engineering company who wished to reach key manufacturing decision makers.
- Does the seminar have the right degree of authority? If the manufacturing seminar was organized by an official body such as the Department of Trade and Industry, that would add a degree of authority to the presenting companies.
- Do the other seminar presentations complement your message and reinforce the partnership theme?
- Will the seminar format provide you with enough time to present your arguments in detail? If not, how easily can you follow up the seminar audience?

There are a number of important actions to be taken to ensure that the seminar meets your communications objectives:

- Set specific objectives for the seminar, for example, to raise awareness of the importance of partnership.
- Select speakers with the authority and status to present strategic messages.
- Ensure that the presentation focuses on concerns and business issues that are important to your customers.
- Incorporate the positioning messages that stress the strategic benefits of partnership. These are described later in this chapter.

Using the example of the fictitious 'Manufacturing in the 1990s" seminar, this is an example of how an engineering company might utilize the seminar to reach key contacts in industry.

'Manufacturing in the 1990s' is run by an independent conference organizer in conjunction with a government body such as the Department of Trade and Industry. The organizers have assembled a group of presenters from industry, government and the academic world and have invited an audience of senior executives from Britain's leading manufacturing companies. The speakers cover strategically important topics such as new developments in manufacturing technology, the importance of information systems, changing investment criteria and human resource implications of the likely changes. Within the context of the seminar, a presentation on the strategic benefits of partnership is appropriate and helps to provide senior executives with a broad perspective. The seminar positions partnership as an integral element of competitive manufacturing management. The company's paper is presented by the managing director and provides a unique opportunity for high-level contact with other senior executives. After the seminar, the company takes the opportunity to maintain communication by mailing management summaries of the seminar papers to delegates and important customers or prospects who were unable to attend. Telephone research conducted before and after the seminar revealed that awareness of the benefits of partnership had increased by 18 per cent, and this provided a valuable basis for planning the next stage of the communications programme.

Executive briefings on partnership

Executive briefings are similar in many ways to seminars, but they are completely under your control. For example, the briefings can adopt the same format as a seminar, with a number of different speakers from your company presenting on related topics. However, the content of the presentations is completely under your control and can be tailored to the business needs of individual customers. A number of larger organizations have set up special executive briefing centres to concentrate on this important aspect of business development. The briefing centres are often located in converted country houses with full presentation facilities, accommodation, catering and areas for discussion and relaxation. The intention is to create an environment where busy executives can get away from day-to-day pressures and concentrate on issues of strategic importance.

An environment like that is helpful, but not essential. Management briefings can be held on your customers' premises, at your offices or in a conference-type location such as a hotel or business centre. It is, however, important to provide an area where the meeting can take place without disturbance in an atmosphere that is conducive to strategic thinking.

The briefing is designed to bring executives up-to-date with issues that are seen as important to their business and to help them decide how to assess the potential of an issue such as partnership within their organization. The agenda for an executive briefing on partnership might include the following sessions:

- The business benefits of partnership
- How is partnership currently used within the industry?
- Is partnership relevant to your organization?
- The management implications of partnership
- Assessing the potential for partnership
- A timetable and action programme for implementing partnership.

As well as demonstrating your understanding of your customer's business and your willingness to help them improve their business performance, a briefing session can encourage open discussion on your customers' business needs and improve working relationships. The executive briefing gives your customers the opportunity to decide whether they can work comfortably with you and demonstrates that partnership depends on close working relationships and an atmosphere of trust.

To help customers get the optimum benefit from executive briefings, provide them with workbooks, case histories and models to use in planning their own programmes.

Management reports on partnership

Management reports can be issued to different members of the target audience to introduce the concept of partnership. Management reports describe the benefits of partnership and provide an outline of the main issues customers should review when they are considering partnership. Many management reports are based on market research and provide customers with an overview of current practice. A management report is not a promotional publication; it should be written in a neutral tone and it should offer customers objective advice that will help them to make effective decisions. By improving the quality of the decision-making process, you can ensure that your partnership proposals are evaluated professionally. Management reports demonstrate that you understand your own and your partner's business and that you are prepared to help your partners improve the quality of their own decision making.

An information systems company produced a management report on the management implications of just-in-time (JIT) manufacturing processes to ensure that their partners were aware of their own responsibilities. Research had shown that companies who adopted JIT without considering the full potential impact on their business tended to blame their information system for problems that were actually due to lack of understanding and poor management. The management report was structured as a briefing document for different members of the management team. It explained that the JIT approach to manufacturing required the commitment and involvement of the whole management team. JIT decisions were shown to be wide ranging, involving the chief executive and board director, together with managers and executives responsible for production, finance, purchasing and marketing. The report explained the potential benefits of JIT, illustrating them with statistics and conclusions from the information system manufacturer's experience in implementing JIT in its own factories. The report then outlined an agenda for discussing JIT and highlighted the critical management decisions. The report was widely used in manufacturing industry and was adopted as a standard by a number of professional institutes who were trying to improve management standards.

Management reports play an important role in building effective relations with contacts at all levels in the customer organization by promoting informed, thorough discussion of the potential of partnership:

- They demonstrate to senior executives that your partnership proposals have taken their business issues into consideration.
- They help middle managers to make informed decisions about partnership and reduce the risk of poor decision-making that is narrowly focused.
- They can help purchasing executives to take a broader view of the importance of partnership by demonstrating the wide-ranging implications and business benefits that can result.

Corporate public relations

Executive briefings, seminars and management reports help to raise awareness of the benefits of partnership in a direct way, by bringing potential partners face to face, or by promoting informed discussion. However, it may not be possible to reach all your contacts directly, or there may be potential contacts you are not aware of. Corporate public relations can help to increase your coverage of your target market through exposure in appropriate media.

Corporate public relations is a broad subject outside the scope of this book, but the most relevant activities are feature articles or profiles in the business press. The business press covers specialist newspapers such as the *Financial Times*, the business sections of daily and weekly newspapers, business magazines such as *Management Today* and trade magazines specific to your industry such as *Engineering Today*.

Achieving customer focus

Customer focus is an integral part of an integrated marketing campaign. It ensures that the customer is central to all activities and it helps to bring together different messages about the company and its products so that customers recognize the quality of service that they are being offered. Customer focus is primarily concerned with internal communications, but it also permeates through external communications to clarify and reinforce product and marketing messages. Internal communications should be structured to build understanding in all the departments which contribute to customer care. These might include:

- Design
- Manufacturing
- Distribution
- Sales and marketing
- Administration
- Accounts.

Many of these departments do not feel that they contribute directly to customer focus, but their role is vital in ensuring overall customer satisfaction. The communications programme begins at the recruitment stage when recruitment advertisements spell out corporate policy on customer care:

- Recruitment advertisements and recruitment literature should stress that the company is committed to the highest standards of customer care and that each individual is responsible for achieving corporate standards and contributing to overall corporate success. These recruitment messages can help to build confidence in employees that they have an important role to play in the success of the company and this helps to build awareness and commitment throughout an organization.
- Training literature and programmes should also reflect the importance of customer care and explain that training is available to each employee to improve standards.

- To help employees understand the importance of customer service and the practical implications of customer focus programmes, customer satisfaction guides should be issued to all employees. These describe the main problems faced by customers and explain their main concerns about the service that should be provided. The guide should also describe the most important elements of customer service and the standards which apply.
- Motivation programmes can help to maintain high levels of interest in the customer focus programme and build a high level of commitment to the programme's success. Programmes like the Chairman's Award for Customer Excellence reward high achievers and give customer service programmes a high profile. They are therefore valuable in building team spirit and a commitment to excellence.
- Customer communications are an integral part of a customer focus programme. They help to make customers aware of the standards of service that are available and demonstrate that the company is committed to quality. For example, a customer charter not only explains a customer's rights, it confirms that the company is committed to high standards.
- Customer care messages can be integrated with other marketing communications in a simple way, 'We care about our customers' or they can form the basis of complete campaigns. Boots' recent 'Who cares' campaign presented the caring approach across a wide range of products and services and is a good example of integrated marketing and customer care messages. The customer care messages are not simply tagged onto the end of advertisements or commercials, they are integral to the whole campaign.
- Customer care programmes which provide customer offers or services designed to overcome specific problems or objectives. In the automotive market, for example, programmes such as courtesy car claim to offer customers the highest levels of convenience and are presented in a way that demonstrate the dealers' commitment to quality service. Different aftercare services can be integrated with a common theme of customer care and unified with an approach such as services for peace of mind.
- Information about customer service standards and customer care programmes can be conveyed to customers through press information and through direct marketing to key opinion formers. When the Post Office was relocating main post offices to out of town sites or to instore locations they presented the changes as a major advance in customer service and tried to ensure that opinion formers understood the key issues behind the changes.

Communicating customer care and customer focus requires a wide-ranging integrated communications programme which will not only influence the people who deliver customer service, but also the customers who benefit from customer care and the people who influence public opinion.

Managing change

When business goes through a major change, a clear, consistent, integrated communications strategy is vital. Change creates an atmosphere of uncertainty and it is vital that everyone understands the important issues and feels that they can contribute to the success of a change. Change can come about for a number of reasons:

- Introduction of new technology
- Changes in working practice
- Marketing or competitive changes
- Organizational change that impacts on the role of individuals or whole departments
- Changes in ownership or management structure.

Changes like this can have an impact on different groups of people, including employees, customers, shareholders, distributors and suppliers, so it is essential that an integrated communications programme deals with the concerns of individual groups. At the centre of the programme is a communications strategy that explains the positive benefits of the changes.

Take as an example the takeover of one manufacturer by another. It is critical to the long-term success of the new organization that change is communicated effectively and that all parties respond favourably to the change.

- Corporate advertising. If the takeover involves major organizations, corporate advertising in the financial and business press can be important in raizing awareness of the benefits of the change. Corporate advertisements would reach important decision makers as well as investors. However, corporate advertisements can only outline the major issues and present benefits in general terms.
- Press information must be carefully controlled to ensure that readers develop a full understanding of the key issues. Press briefing packs, interview programmes and news updates can help to achieve high levels of awareness and understanding at the beginning of the process. As the merger develops and

changes occur in the structure of the new company, regular news releases and feature articles can help to build a profile of the new organization.

- Internal communications are one of the most important elements of the communications mix at this stage. Uncertainty about jobs, future plans and the direction of the new organization can destroy morale and act as a barrier to the progress of the new merger. Staff briefings, information packs, magazines and other publications describing the rationale of the new organization can all help to build understanding of the new organization. There are also key influencers within the organization – management groups, trades unions and key employees – who can form the target of a direct marketing campaign. These key influencers can help to develop a communications channel throughout the organization and spread important messages.

- The salesforce are a particularly important group here because they are in direct contact with customers and their influence should not be underestimated. Salesforce briefings should focus on the important business benefits of the merger to the company, the customer and the salesforce themselves. A pocket guide to essential facts about the merger provides useful guidelines and ensures that messages are presented consistently.

- Customer communications need to reassure customers that they remain the most important focus of the company. Customers fear that continuity of support may be lost or that quality may change. Major customers who have built a dependent relationship with a strategic supplier will have concerns that they may not be able to sustain the relationship and protect their supply base. Customer communications should therefore be handled at a dual level – generic communications through channels such as press relations and corporate advertising, and direct marketing which explains in specific terms how individual business relationships are likely to change. This direct marketing programme might also include briefing sessions with key customer groups which enable them to meet important members of the new management team and to discuss their individual cases through question and answer sessions.

- The financial community play an important role in ensuring the smooth acceptance and transition of a merger. Stockbroker briefings, corporate brochures, financial press relations and press relations activities which bring financial journalists and investors together with members of the new management team can help to build better understanding of the new developments.

- Suppliers and distributors, like employees, need to understand their role in the new environment. They are concerned that business relationships will change and that their own business could be affected by the changes. As well as general information on the rationale and benefits of the merger, they also need individual briefings on the way the relationship is likely to develop.

Change is rarely simple and this section only outlines the complex communications process that needs to take place to ensure that change is handled successfully. Change may not always be driven by something as significant as a merger. Organizational changes or the introduction of new technology can have a significant impact on employees, customers, suppliers and distributors, so it is vital that they are thoroughly briefed. Change can be a powerful positive factor rather than a cause for concern and change can demonstrate that an organization is committed to improvement and progress. In any business relationship, information on change can play an important role in indicating progress. Information, training and clear explanation help to ensure that any change is implemented successfully. Failure to implement change can mean a poor return on investment, lost business opportunities and a negative attitude which does not help the company to operate efficiently.

Improving local marketing performance

Companies who market their products or services through distributors, retail outlets or third parties depend on effective local performance to ensure the overall success of their marketing strategy. Improving the consistency of customer service and achieving local marketing impact can help to establish a national marketing policy and build successful sales in every sector of the market. Integrated communications programmes operate at a number of different levels:

- Explaining the franchise opportunity to gain full commitment and understanding from the local network and attracting new outlets to increase coverage.
- Product and marketing information to ensure that local outlets can carry out an effective local marketing operation.
- Marketing support material to help local outlets operate their own local marketing programmes.

- Joint marketing programmes to target specific customers or improve overall performance.
- Customer focus programmes which raise awareness of customer service and provide incentives for local outlets to deliver the highest standards of customer service.
- Customer communications to explain the benefits of working with an efficient local network.
- Ongoing communications to ensure that local outlets are kept up-to-date with all aspects of the organization and its service.

Together, these communications activities will help distributors and manufacturers to work together to improve local marketing performance.

Franchise opportunities

The franchise opportunity is an important way to build commitment and ensure that a local network operates effectively. This would include information on the product's position in the marketplace, the scope of the network, operating standards and the profit potential of operating as a franchised distributor. It would include extensive operating information and could be linked to administrative and support material. The introductory material would include important positioning messages about the current success of the manufacturer and would feature key strengths of the product or service. The local marketing pack would also include information on the full marketing support programme available.

Product and marketing information

This would reinforce the messages in the launch pack and would give local outlets all the information they need to market the product successfully. Published information would be fully integrated with the training available from the manufacturer and should be carefully targeted to the individual needs of the local outlet. Within an overall network, the number and size of outlets can vary considerably so it is important to match support and information to the needs of the outlet. A research programme which identified the business needs of each outlet was used to build a database for mailing local market information and also helped to build a valuable partnership with individual outlets. Because the information was tailored to the needs of individual outlets, each outlet was able to develop business to its own potential. The marketing information would also include full information on current support campaigns, providing comprehensive guidelines on operating local marketing campaigns.

Marketing support

This type of material is tailored to the needs of local outlets and is fully integrated with national marketing programmes so that the creative themes are used consistently across both national and local campaigns. To ensure that marketing support is used effectively the guide also includes valuable information on agency services and the procedures for obtaining support material and operating local campaigns.

Joint marketing programmes

These are a valuable form of support which boosts the distributor marketing effort and helps to ensure consistent effort at both national and local level.

Customer focus programmes

These are an important method of improving overall local standards and helping to provide customers with a consistent national service. This consistency of service is vital to retaining customers within a national network and branding the network. A chain of retail outlets for example can be branded in the same way as a product, but customers need to know that they will enjoy the same standards of service wherever they go in the network. Petrol stations, supermarkets or convenience food outlets can be strongly branded so that the company can advertise them on a national scale. Consistent standards can be achieved by implementing national standards based on customer research. For example, a network might impose customer focus standards which cover the main requirements such as opening hours, convenience, location, price, range of offers and other factors. These customer focus standards can be imposed as part of the franchise agreement or they can be introduced voluntarily with the backing of an incentive and motivation programme. The incentive programme would be used to recognize excellence in customer service and could be structured so that it reflected the most important elements of customer service. A regional programme with national finals helps to encourage a sense of team spirit and focuses the entire local network on the importance of local standards.

Ongoing communications

A programme of ongoing communications is vital to the long-term development of a local network. It is easy to have initial enthusiasm and to hit the high points during the emotional challenge of a product launch, but it is more difficult to sustain enthusiasm during the longer term.

Local outlets can play a crucial role in developing business on a national scale, but it is vital that local and national activity are fully integrated. National advertising and marketing can be used to develop powerful brand propositions but local marketing support must be carefully targeted and focused on local needs.

Effective product support

Product support is the most widely used application of integrated marketing. The full range of communications techniques can be utilized but they must be carefully related to reflect the marketing objectives. New product launches are crucial to the success of a business - they reflect a considerable amount of investment and represent a high profile activity that can signal corporate success or failure. A product launch pulls together all the elements and demands an intensive effort to get the programme through successfully.

Internal communications

Internal communications are vital to the early success of the programme: the new product development team must sell its concepts to the senior management team who will commit resources to the project. They also need to win the support of a number of departments who will form part of the product launch process – manufacturing, design, research and development, distribution and marketing. Each of these departments needs to be aware of the scope and benefits of the programme so that they can make their own effective contribution.

Sales and marketing departments who will be involved in the practical launch of the product should be fully briefed on the implications of the product so that they can develop their own plans and begin the external communications process. Sales staff, for example, should be issued with comprehensive sales and marketing guides so that they can understand the key benefits of the new product and identify the most important prospects. The marketing department will utilize the specification and objectives of the programme to formulate other marketing programmes and identify the most important sectors for development. When the product is fully developed an internal launch is needed to gain the full commitment of the salesforce and distributor network. The launch event will highlight the strategic importance of the product and develop high levels of interest before the product is introduced to customers.

The internal launch should be fully supported with product and marketing information to help the team sell the product. Launch packs would include comprehensive information on the support programme that will be used to launch the product – the advertising campaigns, direct marketing and customer launch events. The pack would also include details of timing and the overall scale of the programme together with key launch objectives.

To ensure an effective introduction for the new product, the campaign would include a sales and distributor incentive programme which would help to generate high levels of initial interest. Incentives to build high levels of launch stock are essential to giving the coverage vital for a successful consumer launch. If a product is not available in the retail outlets any consumer launch material would be wasted.

The consumer launch can be achieved in number of different ways – national advertising, direct marketing, trial offers, exhibitions, or other forms of marketing which are all designed to raise initial awareness and get consumers to try the new product. National advertising, for example, will provide a high profile launch platform and demonstrate that the company is committed to innovation. National advertising support provides the emotional appeal that product launches need, but may not be able to provoke the kind of action needed for an effective launch.

Sales promotion

Sales promotion activities designed to encourage sampling and product trial are an integral part of the launch process. Curiosity value and novelty are not sufficient to ensure the success of a campaign like this. The promotional campaign must incorporate strong consumer benefits together with an incentive to buy which might include money off or free offers which encourage consumers to take advantage.

Direct marketing

Direct marketing to key consumer groups will allow the marketing group to target their most important prospects with special offers or up-to-date information on the company's performance. A company making complex high technology products might consult with its customers before finalizing the product. Customers would be invited to comment on the new product and to provide their own input so that the product could be customised for specific market sectors or individual customers.

Point-of-sale

Consumer information at the point-of-sale is essential to reaching the prospects and customers who may have been missed in the national advertising campaign. The point-of-sale material can also be used to reinforce other media and complement these with direct response vehicles.

Press information

A strong press information programme will ensure that the new product receives good coverage in the right publications and reaches important members of the target audience. Tie-in promotions with important publications can strengthen the impact even further. For example, reader offers or competitions tied to editorial can provide an initial indication of interest or give information which can be suitable for database development.

Communicating quality

Quality, like customer focus, is an activity that permeates the whole of an organization. Total Quality Management and concepts like Business Process Re-Engineering are helping to transform organizations so that they are more competitive and more profitable. However, they involve considerable change and, without effective communications, both can fail. A strategic plan to implement quality processes must contain an assessment of the communications requirements and an integrated programme that achieves the highest levels of commitment and understanding. There are a number of important stages:

- Providing a vision
- Leading from the top
- Developing champions
- Communicating the programme to staff
- Maintaining the programme
- Communicating quality to customers.

Providing a vision

Introducing quality can be a fragmented process or a grand scheme. In manufacturing companies, quality control and inspection are an established part of the manufacturing process, so staff may wonder why the process is being extended to other business activities. Why should an accounts department or a design group or a salesforce be responsible for quality. Quality is a departmental function. Without an overall strategy, quality is reduced to a routine production task.

ICL saw the importance of a vision when they built their quality programme and their internal communications around the concept of the 'ICL Way'. It was a simple phrase, but it formed part of every communication and it implied that every activity had to be a quality activity. The graphic device was simple – a tick – a recognized quality symbol, but sheer weight of use gave it added value and strength.

Ford launched their internal and external communications programme with a vision of total quality that would extend throughout the supply chain. The programme was supported by a vision 'Quality First' which was also used by sub-contractors to put together their own quality programmes. The vision was reinforced by another important factor – the supplier group had been rationalized and the remaining suppliers had to comply with the standards to remain on the approved list.

Leading from the top

When programmes like Total Quality Management have such far-reaching implications, it is essential that the programme is led from the top. ICL's Chairman, Peter Bonfield, adopted a high profile during the transformation of ICL to a total quality company. Bonfield led the programme personally – briefing senior management groups, talking to groups of employees, appearing in videos and using every public relations opportunity to raize the profile of the quality programme. Interviews with Bonfield were replayed on the corporate video network and in employee magazines, as well as customer publications. Bonfield put quality on the corporate agenda and demonstrated a personal commitment to its success.

Developing champions

The leader cannot achieve all the communications objectives alone, so it is essential that other people can take on the role of filtering the message through the organization. Management commentators call these people champions. Their task is to utilize communications media to build commitment and enthusiasm for change. Champions make frequent presentations, they hold briefing meetings, they are regular contributors to employee magazines and they take personal responsibility for the motivation and incentive programmes that drive the changes forward.

Communicating programmes to staff

The first three phases rely largely on personal performance and the communications are likely to use live media – presentations, briefings and videos. The detailed communication of the programme uses conventional written media. ICL's communications programme began with an audit of the staff who were essential to the success of the programme - which departments and which individuals within those departments were crucial to success. The audit asked how aware those contacts were of the quality issues and reviewed the communications aimed at them. The audit identified the crucial communications tasks and enabled ICL to target their internal communications.

This 'building' stage was crucial with brochures, videos and magazine articles setting out the overall aims of the programme. Individual quality binders were given to key staff and staged communications used to build increasing commitment. Using printed communications, it was easier to maintain consistent communications standards – each detailed communications piece included positioning messages as well as the specific messages.

Maintaining the programme

Although a large part of the internal communications budget is used to launch and implement a programme like this, it is just as important to maintain high levels of interest. A programme needs to be refreshed to ensure that staff continue to maintain the same standards. Incentive and motivation programmes can be used to rebuild awareness, for example including quality recognition programmes that reward high-performing employees and encourage all-round performance can create much wider interest. A broadly based incentive programme which rewards team performance combined with regular programme communications will provide the push to lift a quality programme to new levels.

Communicating quality to customers

Although Total Quality Management is an internal process, it is just as important that customers are aware of the company's progress. Many companies utilize the fact that they are seeking accreditation under an independent standard like BS 5750 to demonstrate their commitment to quality. Approval under an independent standard is a sure sign to customers that a company is seeking to provide its customers with a quality solution. When a company is registered the symbol can be used in all communications. Quality registration is a key element in corporate communications persuading customers that the company can provide the highest level of product and service consistency.

Quality has an important role to play in business-to-business where companies build their new business pitch around a quality focus. An integral part of the quality process is customer feedback and communications can be utilized to encourage the right level of feedback. Customer communications would explain the important role that the customer plays in the quality process by evaluating the product and letting the supplier know how it meets their requirements. In that way customers can help suppliers refine their quality processes. Quality communications reflect the same considerations as partnership communications – getting the customer involved in the supply process.

Summary

Although integrated marketing is primarily used to support products, it can also be used to achieve key building objectives such as improving sales performance, building partnership, achieving customer focus, managing change, improving local marketing performance, providing effective product support and communicating quality. By delivering the highest standards of communications, an organization strengthens its own competitive performance.

6 Campaigns in action

Introduction

This chapter looks at integrated marketing in action by reviewing a range of different campaigns from consumer, business, and service sectors. Although the campaigns are fictitious, they are based on real examples. The campaigns include:

- Position a new car model as value for money
- Broaden the market for a hi-fi system
- Develop sales of a regional fast food chain
- Introduce a new food product to a regional test market
- Build the loyalty of high-spending telephone users
- Launch a 'shop' concept for a petrol retailer
- Increase customer retention for a life assurance company
- Develop sales for a chain of booksellers
- Launch computer software into a new business sector
- Increase traffic for a regional business airline
- Demonstrate through-life benefits for an engineering component.

Position a new car model as value for money

This model from a volume car manufacturer competes in the small family saloon class. In terms of price, performance and features, it is competitive with other models in the sector. However, to differentiate it from competitors, the key proposition to consumers is low cost of ownership.

The manufacturer markets through a national network of franchised dealerships. The campaign must therefore concentrate on marketing the concept to dealerships as well as the consumer. Failure to achieve dealership commitment could ruin the impact of a consumer campaign at the point-of-sale.

Consumer advertising

Consumer advertising in national and regional press and television stresses the concept of value for money by highlighting low cost of ownership benefits such as fuel economy, longer service intervals, simplicity of servicing and repair, and the availability of low-cost finance. Consumers are invited to call a freephone number to request a brochure or ask for further information.

Dealer customer direct marketing

Existing dealership customers who fit the consumer profile for the new model are mailed with an information pack and video which explain the concept of value for money. As an incentive to take a test drive, they are offered a choice of free motoring accessories, further reinforcing the concept of value for money.

Dealership launch material

To ensure that the network is fully committed to the new programme each dealership receives a detailed product briefing and launch pack at a series of regional business meetings. The launch pack explains how to communicate the concept to customers and prospects and describes the launch support material available. The pack contains support material for sales, service and parts departments who will all be involved in marketing the concept to consumers. A guide for the sales team explains the different value for money features and describes how to present those features to prospects.

Dealership promotional material

Posters, display modules and other point-of-sale material reinforce the messages of the consumer advertising campaign within the dealership. An audio tape describing how dealership service helps to maintain low cost of ownership through scheduled servicing and competitive parts and repair costs is given to every consumer who buys a new car.

After-sales follow-up

A series of direct marketing programmes is used to maintain contact with customers and reinforce the concept of value for money after the sale. The campaign includes low-cost servicing vouchers to encourage customers to use the dealership service operations, do-it-yourself workshops to encourage customers to carry out routine service tasks themselves and guidelines on economical motoring.

Summary

The campaign ensures that there are no weak links in communication between the manufacturer and the customer. The impact of the consumer campaign could have been wasted if it had not been followed up effectively at dealership level.

Broaden the market for a hi-fi system

The manufacturer has an established reputation for quality hi-fi systems and holds a strong market share in a high-price sector. However, the manufacturer is aware that low-price competitors are opening up a wider market by making hi-fi more accessible and more affordable for consumers who might have only considered a basic audio system. The manufacturer wants to protect share and margins in the traditional market, but take advantage of the broader opportunities.

The strategy is to use the established reputation to brand the lower price range, and also demystify hi-fi for the new generation of buyers. The new product range will be marketed initially through popular electrical retailers, leaving the established brands with traditional dealers. However, in the long term, the manufacturer aims to market the whole range through traditional dealers to encourage consumers to trade up to higher price products.

Press advertising

National press advertising highlights the affordable hi-fi concept and stresses the brand heritage to reassure consumers that they will have a quality product. Consumers are invited to call a freephone number to request a brochure and get the name of their nearest retailer.

Direct marketing follow-up

Respondents are mailed with the offer of taking part in a free prize draw to win a collection of compact discs, whether they buy a system or not. As part of the data capture process, prospects are asked to provide details of their current audio systems and musical tastes. Future mailings can be highly targeted with offers of musical or event promotions that reflect the consumer's tastes.

Retail sales development

To ensure that prospects get the right level of service when they visit a retail outlet, the manufacturer provides product training for retail staff. The training covers the main features and benefits of hi-fi systems and tells sales staff how to explain them in non-technical terms that will not intimidate a prospect who just wants to listen to music. To encourage sales staff to sell the product, an incentive programme will operate, offering twenty sales staff a trip to a great musical location such as Vienna, New York or Sydney.

Retail support

Retailers are provided with point-of-sale material that reflects the consumer advertising themes of affordable hi-fi. Brochures on 'making the most of hi-fi' are available and a 'free CD' offer runs for selected periods. Retailers also have access to a central telemarketing service and this is used to follow up respondents to the initial advertising campaign. Participating retailers can run competitions offering prospects the chance to win free concert tickets if they request a demonstration of the hi-fi system.

Customer information

To maintain the theme of accessible hi-fi, customers receive instructions and product guides in a simple, easy-to-use form. Technical terms are out and the guides are designed to ensure that customers are fully satisfied with their systems. A 24-hour helpline is available to any customer who needs advice.

Summary

The campaign ensures that hi-fi is presented as a straightforward accessible product from the outset. The manufacturer ensures that prospects will not be blinded by science at the retail outlet and provides help and guidance after the sale.

Develop sales of a regional fast food chain

A chain of fast food restaurants is expanding its local network on a region by region basis. Customers are offered a quality product with free home delivery within set times and a guarantee of money back if they are not completely satisfied.

In each location, the new outlet will be competing with other types of branded fast food outlet and with local suppliers. The outlets are franchised and, as part of the agreement, the franchise holder must adhere to the company's quality standards. Integrated marketing support is provided centrally to ensure consistency across the network.

Regional and local advertising

Regional press, local press and local commercial radio are the main media for raising consumer awareness of the new outlets. Radio commercials include a freephone number to obtain details of the nearest branch and request introductory vouchers. The press advertisements include the name of all the branches in the area and also include coupons. Poster sites outside cinemas, clubs and other entertainment venues are used to attract customers for late-night specials.

Customer loyalty programmes

Data capture through the freephone number and through coupon information is used as the basis for mailing customers with money-off vouchers and special offers for regular customers. Telemarketing is used selectively to offer frequent buyers a complimentary meal. Customers are also given a hotline number to call in the event of a problem and they are asked to complete occasional questionnaires on the quality of service.

Staff motivation programmes

To ensure that each branch delivers the right level of customer service, branches are measured on their performance. Information from the customer questionnaires and the hotline is used to assess branch performance against targets and selected staff from the best performing branches qualify for a trip to an international convention.

Summary

The campaign combines consumer awareness with high levels of customer service and loyalty building programmes that attract new prospects and retain them as regular customers.

Introduce a new food product to a regional test market

A manufacturer of branded food products is introducing a new Indian dish in a regional test market. The product will form part of a range of speciality foods that will take the manufacturer into new market sectors. The product will be sold through retail outlets that currently stock the manufacturer's range as well as speciality food stores where distribution is currently weak.

The marketing programme will therefore concentrate on improving levels of distribution as well as achieving sales.

Regional television advertising

Regional television slots, tied in with food and 'family' programmes, is used to raise awareness of the product and demonstrate to retailers the potential levels of marketing support. The TV campaign includes an offer of an Indian cookbook through a freephone number. The book is available at a special price and is available on proof of purchase.

Retailer promotional support

Retailers are provided with a local advertising service that includes promotional offers of free meals at a local Indian restaurant, together with a prize draw for a holiday for two in India. The manufacturer also provides point-of-sale material that reflects the different promotional campaigns that are running.

Money-off first purchase coupons are available for local distribution and retailers can also take advantage of a direct mail service that builds on the local database generated through the television campaign responses. Direct mail is used to make a selection of special offers based on different levels of purchase and also provides a basis for direct marketing of future products in the range.

Wholesale and retail incentive programmes

The television advertising and the promotional programmes are an important element in winning distribution. They demonstrate to the retailer that the manufacturer is prepared to back the product with consumer marketing activity that will build high levels of sales. To encourage retailer loyalty, the company also operates an incentive scheme that offers retailers themed prizes and awards for different levels of purchase, from weekend breaks with food from a selection of Indian restaurants to holidays in India.

Summary

The campaign builds distribution and raises customer awareness at the same time. Themed promotions help to support the original advertising campaign, while database development forms the basis for direct marketing of future range extensions.

Build the loyalty of high-spending telephone users

A telephone company has identified competitive threats to a sector of its customer base that are heavy telephone users. These are people whose bills exceed a certain level and who may use their telephone for both domestic and business purposes.

Database development

To find out more about these customers and to plan a direct marketing campaign, the company mails out a questionnaire with an incentive to return of a free phone card. Although the company already knows the customer's level of spend through its billing process, the questionnaire is designed to find out how customers use their phone – how many people, what sort of calls, and information on business usage.

Loyalty programmes

As a first stage, the customers are offered a volume-related discount on their quarterly bills in return for an annual fee. Each customer has a personal illustration of the potential savings based on recent billing information. The customer is also offered the opportunity to participate in an award programme which provides points for telephone usage. The points can be redeemed for gifts from a collector catalogue and this may also encourage increased use.

Direct marketing

The database can also be used as a basis for targeted mailings to customers with specific interests. For example, customers who indicate that they make large numbers of international calls can be kept up-to-date with developments in international services, while small business users can be mailed with information on business products or services. Naturally, telemarketing is used extensively to follow up mailings and obtain feedback from customers on the new type of service.

Summary

This programme includes elements that help to identify the needs of individual customers and follows it up with communications that are precisely targeted, as well as loyalty programmes that reward customers for different levels of expenditure.

Launch a 'shop' concept for a petrol retailer

Oil companies see petrol retail outlets as an opportunity to offer a wider range of services to drivers and the local community. By introducing a convenience shop into the outlet, they not only increase sales overall but position themselves as part of the local community. The change from petrol station to shop not only requires communications to raise awareness, it also needs training in retailing and customer service skills.

Television and radio advertising to raise consumer awareness

Regional advertising is used to raise awareness while the network is expanding. National campaigns can be used when the network is complete and the service can be positioned as an integral part of the brand. A freephone number is included in the regional campaigns to encourage consumers to ask for a directory of local outlets and to get up-to-date information on new store openings. Local radio advertising is also used to reach drivers from outside the region who might use an outlet while they were passing.

Sales promotion and loyalty campaigns

Door-to-door coupon drops were used to make local customers aware of the shop, while in-store promotions in conjunction with other manufacturers were used to build sales. By integrating awards for retail sales with petrol sales the company was able to build customer loyalty through its 'collector' scheme. The scheme was based on a collector card which enabled the company to profile both customer purchasing patterns and the overall pattern of sales through the outlet.

Staff training and incentive schemes

One of the problems in petrol retailing was the high level of casual staff and staff turnover. Although this did not impact on petrol sales, it could affect the success of the long-term branding of the retail outlets. Staff training and motivation was an important part of the development process, with an emphasis on customer service. Staff uniforms were introduced and a discount purchase scheme operated which gave staff different levels of discount depending on length of service.

Summary

This programme incorporates elements of a long-term branding strategy with tactical sales promotion and customer loyalty programmes to strengthen performance and build a sound customer base.

Increase customer retention for a life assurance company

This life assurance company has a national brand name and an established customer base. However, it identifies that competitors are increasingly concentrating on customer service and building long-term relationships with customers. The new approach is perceived positively by consumers and the company believes that it could lose business if it does not change its own marketing programme which is focused on selling products, rather than dealing with customers.

The transformation will require not only changes in the marketing programme, but a change in internal attitudes, particularly from the salesforce. The company also has to make independent financial advisers aware of the changes, if they are to attract business from that source.

Television and press advertising

National television and press advertising are used to build an overall brand for the company with creative themes that stress the benefits of dealing with one assurance company for a care-free life. Press advertisements include a response coupon for data capture which invites customers to send for more information or contact their local independent financial adviser.

Customer direct marketing

Existing policy holders are mailed with details of the new service initiative. A customer service leaflet explains the new role of the salesforce as consultants and invites the customer to make an appointment for a no-obligation financial health check. Customers are also asked to indicate additional products that they are interested in so that the company can keep them up-to-date on relevant new product information. Customers are also advised that their consultants will keep in regular contact with them to build an understanding of their needs and their changing financial circumstances.

Direct marketing to prospects

Prospects who respond to the advertisements are followed up by direct mail and telemarketing. They are offered a financial health check by a company consultant or put in touch with an independent financial adviser. If they state an interest in specific product areas such as pensions or term assurance, they receive further information together with a series of staged incentives encouraging them to ask for a quotation or make the first premium payments.

Building long-term relationships

The company uses information on the database to plan future campaigns for individual customers. Regular consultation and telephone updates are used to maintain the customer profile, and mailings concentrate on cross-selling other products or selling-up existing products. Product literature is revised to explain the change in approach and reflect consumer advertising themes.

Communicating with sales staff and independent financial advisers

It is important to communicate the change in direction to the people who are dealing direct with customers. The salesforce have traditionally handled specific products or operated on a regional basis and many of them were remunerated on the basis of product sales against target. Their new role as consultants means that they have to provide customers with a much broader service and concentrate on long-term relationships. To reflect this change, remuneration packages are revised and they are given extensive training as consultants. Recruitment advertising stresses this new role and reflects the creative themes of the consumer advertising.

Independent financial advisers receive information on the company's approach to business, together with an explanation of the way this affects the product range.

Summary

This programme is designed to build understanding of the way the company is changing. Customers, sales staff and independent financial advisers receive a detailed explanation of the change. The company also refines its database so that it communicates in a more direct way with customers and prospects in the future.

Develop sales for a chain of booksellers

A chain of bookstores wants to develop a brand image to ensure that customers throughout the country recognize quality of service and choose that store rather than a local bookshop. The company has built high volume sales through brand building, but wants to consolidate its customer base and achieve higher levels of repeat purchase.

National press advertising
The company continues to use national press to build high levels of brand awareness, but now adds a response mechanism for data capture. It develops a number of competitions in conjunction with national newspapers, offering readers the chance to win a £100 book voucher in exchange for completing a questionnaire on reading and book buying habits. The information can be used to identify keen book buyers and forms the basis of future direct marketing programmes.

Loyalty programmes
Database development is the first stage in building customer loyalty. Information on reading habits is used to create targeted mailings that reflect the readers' specific interests. The company develops a small group of 'clubs' segmented in the same way as book clubs. Although members are offered books by mail order, the company maintains their interest in visiting the bookstore by arranging author signing ceremonies and other social events. Regular readers are offered a discount card which they can use with every purchase and they also earn points that qualify them for free books up to a certain value.

Developing high volume sectors
Education remains a key market for booksellers and the company develops its sales to this sector with a range of programmes to retain loyalty. It provides schools and colleges with an information service on course books, which includes reviews of new books, advice on new editions and a special discount service for students.

Summary
This programme continues the branding exercise carried out by the national advertising programme and uses information on frequent users to develop loyalty programmes.

Launch computer software into a new business sector

The company, a leading supplier of business software, has identified an opportunity to market a customised product to the insurance sector. The product includes features and routines that will help insurance companies improve their productivity and standards of customer service by automating many routine clerical tasks.

The product offers considerable benefits over standard packages which have to be customised by IT specialists within insurance companies to provide specialist functions. The marketing programme uses a number of different routes to communicate with the right decision makers. The products are marketed direct to large corporate users and through specialist retailers to smaller customers.

Specialist advertising

Advertising in magazines read by the insurance industry help the company to reach one group of decision makers – the insurance managers who will benefit from using the programme. The advertisement invites readers to request a free management guide to improving productivity in the insurance business. The company also has to influence the IT specialists within insurance companies, but does not use the IT press because of the high levels of wastage.

Direct marketing

Direct marketing can be used to reach the IT specialists and the insurance managers with information on the key benefits of the software and an offer to trade-in existing software packages. The company also provides direct marketing support material to retailers for use in local markets.

Marketing with equipment partners

The software company works in partnership with specialist computer manufacturers who customize units for particular applications. The partners offer customers complete packages of hardware, software that is already loaded on the equipment and service that covers software upgrades and maintenance. The customer has the benefits of one-stop shopping and this approach reinforces the values of the software package.

Summary

The product is marketed through a number of different channels but integrated marketing allows the company to communicate similar benefits to different decision makers and through the marketing programmes used by retailers and equipment partners.

Increase traffic for a regional business airline

The airline operates mainly domestic flights between most major cities, with a small number of short-haul European flights to popular business destinations in Germany, France and the Netherlands. The company competes with larger airlines on the European routes and some of the domestic routes, but faces competition from alternative forms of transport such as rail or road on many of its domestic routes.

The airline adopts a policy of niche marketing, targeting businesses that could benefit from a convenient rapid service between certain destinations. The oil industry, for example, would be heavy users of flights between production centres at Aberdeen and headquarters in London. The marketing strategy is to concentrate on this type of business and develop loyalty among frequent users.

Research

A research programme is used to identify companies with regional offices near the airline's terminals and head offices near other terminals. The company targets business sectors where meetings are important and where executives and other workers are likely to spend a great deal of time on travel.

Specialist advertising

The airline runs advertisements in business publications read by its target market - oil, engineering, accountancy for example – inviting readers to receive a free travel audit. The audit looks at their annual domestic business travel expenditure and includes a proposal for a travel package that could reduce overall costs. The airline also uses advertisements in the business sections of regional newspapers in the catchment area of its terminals to raise awareness of the service that is available.

Direct marketing

To back up the specialist advertising, the company mails information on its services direct to companies in the target market. The companies are offered the travel audit as well as corporate discounts on travel by staff. The direct marketing explains the benefits of using the airline between key destinations and also describes the levels of customer service available.

Building customer loyalty

The loyalty programme operates at two levels – corporate and individual traveller. The corporate programme includes a package of discounts, travel information, management reporting and added-value services such as car hire and hotel bookings which help to reduce the customer's travel administration burden.

At a personal level, travellers are offered the benefits of 'frequent flyer' programmes, including a programme like 'Air Miles' which provides points against distance travelled, the use of exclusive departure lounges and preferential rates on travel-related services such as car hire and accommodation. Information from the frequent flyer programme is fed back into the airline's database to fine-tune future direct marketing to individual or corporate travel patterns.

Summary

This programme makes extensive use of research data to operate a highly-targeted direct marketing programme. The airline avoids head-on confrontation with larger rivals, by targeting niche markets and building individual and corporate loyalty.

Demonstrate through-life benefits for an engineering component

An engineering company developed an advanced composite material that offered designers the advantages of light weight with extremely high strength. The material had been widely used in the aerospace industry but was not yet accepted in general engineering where it was seen as an expensive alternative to traditional materials.

The company developed an integrated campaign that was aimed not just at the designers who specify the material, but the purchasing managers who needed cost justification, and the marketing staff and senior executives who would be convinced of the competitive benefits the material could offer their company.

Specialist press information

This was an innovative material that required a great deal of customer education before acceptance. The company commissioned a series of articles showing how the materials had been used to achieve new performance levels in different engineering sectors. Readers were invited to send for a designer's guide that included the case studies. The press programme ran in specialist engineering and design magazines.

Designer's guide

This was a key element in the whole campaign and was mailed to designers and engineers in prospect companies. The guide explained how to tackle a wide range of current engineering problems using the new material and offered designers the opportunity to discuss their projects with a technical specialist. As an incentive to specify the material, designers were offered a special computer-aided-design software package at discount price. The software was pre-programmed with many of the calculations the designers would have to make when using the new material. The company also set up a technical hotline to provide designers with advice and guidance on new projects.

Direct marketing to other decision makers

Purchasing executives, senior executives and marketing directors in target companies were mailed a management report which outlined the cost-benefits of the new material. It explained how the material, although initially more expensive than traditional engineering materials, would reduce future maintenance costs, improve product performance and increase customer satisfaction. The 'through-life costs' would give the company a significant advantage. The company offered to hold a management workshop for customers to review potential benefits to the company.

Summary

This programme has concentrated on customer education as a means of overcoming initial resistance to the product. It concentrates the marketing effort not just on the immediate user of the product, but on the other decision makers who could influence choice.

7 Customer contact strategies

Introduction

This chapter explains the importance of regular communications with your customers. It stresses the importance of carrying out regular communications audits to see how well key decision makers understand you and describes a number of techniques for maintaining contact, including:

- Direct marketing
- Product updates
- Technical/research updates
- Customer team briefings on corporate progress
- Corporate/financial information
- Company direction
- Customer satisfaction surveys
- Customer performance review meetings
- Customer account team manuals.

Integrated marketing plays an important role in ensuring that every contact with the customer is consistent and high quality.

Carrying out a communications audit

This is an audit of the planned and current communications between an information systems company and its largest client. It is concerned with the relationship and image of the supplier from the customer's point of view. It compares the customer's views with those of the supplier and incorporates the customer's views of competitors. The audit compares the actual perceptions against current communications activities and highlights key communications actions needed to achieve the target perception.

Summary of audit

This is the management summary of the findings of the audit.

The company is setting out to improve the value, market share and quality of its business with this key account, increasing market share from 19 to 25 per cent. To achieve this, the company must secure strategic supplier status and enter a significant collaboration agreement with the customer.

Over the last year the company has improved its image within the key account, but competitors have made further gains. In certain areas the company is highly regarded, but research shows that the customer's senior managers are not aware of the company's current improvement programme. At worst, this means that the company may not be considered for certain major projects and, at best, the company may start at a disadvantage compared with its competitors. The company needs to develop a preference for its products and services, especially in the key areas identified for future business. A strong image development programme will be required to change the attitudes of the customer's senior management team.

This is a summary of the company's current image position:

- The company is almost as 'visible' as its competitors, but is only rated third in all issues associated with image.
- Contact with the customer at all levels is less than professional. According to the customer, the company does not understand its business and its products, and does not communicate its future strategies.
- There is a legacy of poor reputation which has largely been overcome by increased product reliability, but the image persists in the minds of the customer's senior management team.
- The company is perceived as offering lower quality and lower performance than competitors, and users are less satisfied than competitive users.
- The company is seen as losing ground with important decision makers.
- The company is identified more clearly than competitors with specific product lines, but is not rated most highly as the potential supplier of those products.
- The company's major weakness is perceived as its narrow product line and lack of expertise in certain areas.

From an image development point of view, there are three major actions needed to ensure future success:

- The reality of improved performance, reliability and value for money must be sustained and improved.
- The professionalism of the company's staff, their knowledge of their products and understanding of the customer's needs must be improved. The quality and effectiveness of all contacts with the customer must be improved dramatically.
- A positive, well managed and consistent image development programme must be put in place to publicize the company's progress to close the gap between perception and reality and to create a preference for the company by presenting the right messages to the right members of the management team.

Changing perceptions

The major perceptions which must be created to achieve the business goals are:

- The company is a professional organization which understands the customer's business needs and can meet them with a wide range of high quality products and services.
- The company is technically successful in major projects, developing total solutions and delivering value for money, on time, every time.
- The company is winning share from its competitors.
- The company is an approved and respected strategic supplier with whom it is safe to place business.
- The company is a successful and financially stable company with a sound management team – a good prospective supplier and business partner.

Communicating professionalism

'The company is a professional organization which understands the customer's business needs and can meet them with a wide range of high quality products and services.' The messages to support this perception include:

- The company is investing £*** in training over the next year.
- The company is organized into market-focused groups to offer the highest standards of service.
- *** staff are dedicated to the customer's business.
- The company is committed to total quality.
- The company has developed a broad product range and a full range of support services.
- The company's products meet international standards.
- The new product development programme is providing innovative new products.

Communicating technical success

'The company is technically successful in major projects, developing total solutions and delivering value for money, on time, every time.' The important messages to support this perception include:

- The company has an established reputation for innovation.
- The company's products have been selected for the following demanding applications.... .
- Customers are saving money by using the company's products.

- The company's products conform to international standards.
- The company has a research and development budget in excess of £*** and has a team of *** highly skilled people dedicated to technical support.

Communicating market success

'The company is winning share from its competitors.' The important messages to support this perception include:

- The company has been selected to provide products and services to the following customers... .
- The company has recently won a major order worth £***.
- The company has been selected as a strategic supplier to the following customers... .
- The company has gained ** % market share in the last year, while competitors have lost ** % share in the last year.

Communicating strategic supplier status

'The company is an approved and respected strategic supplier with whom it is safe to place business'. The important messages to support this perception include:

- The company has been selected as a strategic supplier to the following market-leading customers... .
- The company is collaborating with a major international organization.
- The company meets the following international product and quality standards... .

Communicating corporate stability

'The company is a successful and financially stable company with a sound management team - a good prospective supplier and business partner.' The important messages to support this perception include:

- The company's annual results show ** % growth in orders, revenue and profits.
- The company is expanding.
- The company is a member of the *** international group.
- The company is the leading European supplier.

The audit has identified the key areas for improving communications performance and it is essential that these messages should be communicated consistently in every form of contact with the customer.

Communications strategy

The remainder of this chapter looks at different techniques for communicating with the customer.

Direct marketing

Direct marketing is used to send targeted communications to named individuals. On a key account, these might be important members of the decision-making team who cannot be contacted directly or who require specific information. Direct marketing can take the form of direct mail letters, brochures, management guides or other publications that meet the reader's main concerns. Direct marketing can also be used to make special promotional offers to named individuals – invitations to seminars, offers of reprints of technical articles, free copies of business briefing guides and other items that enhance your credibility as a supplier. A direct marketing programme is based on planned, regular communications to ensure that each decision maker holds a favourable perception of your company. A programme targeting the technical director aims to position the company as an innovative, technically-advanced supplier. The programme might include:

- Reprints of published articles by technical specialists on your staff.
- A briefing and update on your latest research programme.
- An independent review of your product performance.
- Invitations to a seminar sponsored by your company on industry developments.

By looking at the information requirements of the key decision makers, you can develop a comprehensive direct marketing programme.

Product updates

It is vital that your customers' technical and purchasing specialists always have the latest information on your products. This is not only sound marketing practice, it alerts them to any new developments that may help them to develop their own products. You can use a formal system of change control to ensure that each of your contacts is kept up-to-date.

Technical/research updates

These are similar to product updates, but they notify your customers of future developments so that they can incorporate new technology into their own forward programmes. This type of update not only enhances your technical reputation, it helps to build closer working relationships between the technical groups. These updates can be published occasionally or at regular intervals, say quarterly or annually.

Customer team briefings on corporate progress

Significant developments such as new investment programmes, acquisitions, changes in management, expansion programmes or new product launches are of major interest to your key account customers. By bringing together the two teams, you can take the opportunity to update everyone of the progress and ensure that there are experts on hand to deal with specific issues.

Corporate/financial information

Although financial information is an integral element of the team briefing process, you can keep individual decision makers up-to-date by sending copies of corporate brochures, financial results and other corporate information. A regular flow of information will ensure that key influencers are aware of your financial performance and remain confident of your ability as a stable supplier.

Company direction

It is important that your key customers understand the future direction of your company – how you see your business in the medium and long term, what new developments you plan to introduce, and whether you are considering any fundamental changes to your business. They need to be convinced that you will remain committed to the success of their business and that they will continue to benefit from working closely with you. An understanding of your future direction helps your customers plan their own development.

Customer satisfaction surveys

As well as keeping customers informed of developments in your company, it is also important to monitor their attitudes to your company and your performance on their account. Customer satisfaction surveys are covered in more detail later in the book, but they should be an integral element of a two-way communications strategy.

Customer performance review meetings

As well as measuring customer satisfaction, you should be prepared to review your performance with your key customers and discuss measures for improving performance. By taking a proactive attitude to performance measurement, you demonstrate high levels of customer care and improve relationships with team members. Review meetings can be held at a number of different levels:

- Monthly progress meetings on technical and commercial matters, involving specialist members of the team.
- Quarterly review meetings on overall performance. Most of the team will participate and the meeting will be used to identify any remedial actions needed.
- Annual reviews involving senior members of the team to review performance and discuss key objectives for the coming year.

Customer account team manuals

In a key account environment where a large number of people are involved, an account team manual can be extremely useful. The manual should include all the information needed to operate the account, and would be distributed to members of both teams. The contents of the manual might include:

- Introductory section on the general benefits of working together, focusing on the opportunities to improve business performance and maintain a competitive edge
- The key performance measurements used to assess progress
- The scope of the account relationship, including supply and distribution arrangements, action programmes and levels of technical and marketing cooperation
- An outline of the direction in which the account could develop, including a growth path and possible action programmes
- The quality processes and feedback mechanisms that would be used to control the programme
- The skills and resources of both companies
- The organization of the two companies, including appropriate personnel details
- The responsibilities of both parties and the reporting procedures
- Contact information explaining the communications links between the two companies and the sources of information within each
- Escalation procedures to deal with any problems on the account
- A summary of the main benefits and long-term objectives of the account relationship.

The manual is a valuable technique for building understanding and maintaining relationships between the two parties. It ensures that everyone understands their role and shows how the relationship can be utilized to provide benefits for both parties.

Summary

Regular communication with customers is essential to the success of long-term marketing success. However, the communications programme must be based on carefully-researched information needs. A communications audit can help you to assess attitudes towards your company and provides the basis for planning a communications strategy. Direct marketing can be used to ensure that individual decision makers receive the information they need, while product and technical updates ensure that your customers are kept fully informed on your technical performance. Regular briefings on corporate and financial developments build confidence and ensure that your company is regarded as a stable supplier. It is also important to assess customer attitudes to your performance and discuss improvement programmes through a series of regular team progress meetings. Regular customer contact programmes should be fully integrated.

8 Agency structure

Introduction

This chapter looks at the role of the integrated marketing consultancy. As the earlier part of the book explained, the most important aspect of integrated marketing is that it is channelled through a single source, with a lead agency handling all above and below the line activities or coordinating the work of specialist suppliers with creative control and quality-controlled project management.

Although the single agency structure is perhaps the only effective solution for integrated marketing, a number of organizations have reached compromise situations by maintaining a main above the line agency and coordinating all below the line activities through a second agency working in close cooperation with the above the line agency.

There have been other attempts at providing a complete solution rather than an integrated solution with above the line agency groups setting up subsidiary companies to provide specialist services to clients – a form of one-stop shopping but without the vital ingredient of integration. Other design-based groups have grown through acquisition and merger to include companies in all marketing services disciplines. Through organizational structure or group politics, they too have failed to make the key move and offer the client a truly integrated service. Attempts at referring clients to other services within the group have been thwarted with individual agencies protecting their interests and jealously guarding their own clients.

The move by KMM to establish the UK's first integrated marketing agency took the agency business by surprise but it has set an example that other agencies are now attempting to follow. Kevin Morley's own experience in Rover as a main board director with responsibility for marketing put him in a unique position to see the problems of fragmentation from the client's point of view.

Rover was a classic situation where product managers and marketing services specialists had built up valuable relationships with specialist suppliers who produced marketing support material that had helped to achieve progress. However, there was a feeling that these independent solutions did not present a consistent picture of the Rover Group and its strengths to the consumer. The Rover board also believed that the duplication of effort in dealing with multiple suppliers was an expensive route to producing their campaigns.

Morley's solution was to offer a single integrated solution through a new agency – KMM. KMM would handle all above the line advertising previously handled by an agency and an independent. More importantly, they would also handle all the below the line programmes which had previously been handled on an independent ad hoc basis. Their proposal outlined three major benefits which are a fundamental part of all integrated marketing strategies:

- Integrating all the activities under one creative strategy would strengthen the Rover brand equity.
- Coordinating all marketing activities through a single source would save Rover money.
- Developing integrated campaigns which utilized different media would improve the overall effectiveness of Rover's marketing programmes.

These key benefits of integrated marketing have been discussed and repeated throughout the book and KMM's performance to date has continued to prove the benefits of this approach. KMM's appointment was for a period of five years – a period that both parties felt was important to develop the right sort of working relationship. That period gave Rover the time to rationalize their own marketing activities and to develop new ways of working. It also gave KMM the opportunity to build a structure that would accommodate Rover's changing business needs and provide the quality and continuity of service that would improve Rover's long-term business performance and profitability.

Up to the point of its merger with BMW, Rover had built a leading position in the European car industry with a growth and profit record that was the envy of other automotive manufacturers. Product quality played a vital part in that product transformation, but marketing quality too was a major contributor and results prove that integrated marketing has reduced costs and improved marketing effectiveness.

The KMM structure is the essence of simplicity - one account director is responsible for all communications with the client and the client's own representation has been simplified as much as possible. This ensures that there is no loss of continuity and no conflict of interest between different account groups within the agency. The core team within the agency is:

- Account Director
- Planning Director
- Creative Director.

Together they are responsible for all output on the account and their task is to give overall direction to the account and ensure that every campaign or project achieves its objectives and meets agreed quality standards in terms of standards, budgets, and timing.

Within the agency are creative teams and different groups of marketing services specialists who work under central direction on different aspects of a campaign. Central co-ordination ensures that all the separate projects are working in the same direction and that specialist activities such as direct marketing, telemarketing, advertising and sales support complement each other.

To handle specialist production and to buy in specialist activities that cannot be handled within the agency, KMM work with a group of business partners. These partners work on a long-term basis and work to agreed KMM standards using an independent quality measure such as BS 5750 as a guide. This level of quality control ensures that KMM can offer their clients consistent standards across every aspect of a campaign; this can mean a major reduction in hassle. Anyone who has tried to impose visual standards while working with a broadly based group of suppliers will understand the complexity of this task. KMM suppliers appreciate this approach – as partners they have the opportunity to enjoy long-term continuity – but they are also assured of a comprehensive, practical brief and they are working with clear guidelines.

The other major task for KMM is to handle administration across all these activities and to bill Rover for the comprehensive task. With typical annual billings of around £80 million and a large number of individual transactions, this is a major task, but it has been simplified by the integration of KMM's own computer-based accounting systems with Rover's corporate finance/payment system ISTEL. ISTEL was originally set up to simplify transactions between Rover and its business partners supplying components and services. ISTEL is now an independent operation providing transactions services to many different sectors of industry but its facilities have played a key role in the efficient management of integrated marketing.

This overview of the development and structure of KMM explains the key characteristics of a successful integrated marketing operation. The rest of this chapter looks in more detail at the factors you should use in selecting and working with an integrated marketing agency. It will help you to evaluate current suppliers and assess the potential of agencies to offer a true integrated marketing solution.

Agency structure

An integrated marketing agency must work across all media and understand their relation to each other. An advertising agency which only billed media and depended on commission for its income and profit would find it commercially difficult to offer a totally integrated solution. Its success depends on increasing income from commission.

However, an advertising agency which had below the line subsidiaries within a group structure has the potential to offer an integrated marketing solution. The agency has the specific service skills to offer advice on mixed media solutions but it must have the right operating structure to offer a truly integrated solution. If the client has to deal with different contacts for each specific service there will be a risk of losing continuity and consistency. The group must develop a central coordinator responsible for all client contact.

As the KMM example showed, one account director working with the client works with a single planning/creative team before any specific activity begins. A one-stop shop solution offered by a holding group will only work if the group offers the single contact. The integrated communications agency has a simpler structure that eliminates inter-departmental conflicts – all of the specialists are working within the same agency and they are brought in when it is appropriate by the central coordinating team.

Strategy is developed between the client and the account team and the specialists are brought in to implement it. If the agency does not offer this central point of contact, then it needs to restructure its own organization so that the client gets the benefit of unbiased recommendations. As we mentioned earlier, the key team within an integrated marketing agency includes account director, planning director, creative director and it is worth looking at their role in more detail.

Account Director

The account director is responsible for overall coordination on the account and has the following responsibilities:

- Work with the client to establish overall objectives and develop the strategy.
- Liaise with the client on a day-to-day basis to handle specific campaigns or projects on the client's behalf.
- Develop an agency brief in conjunction with the creative/planning directors.
- Coordinate all agency and external services to fulfil the client's brief and meet overall account objectives.
- Manage the client's budgets across all projects and ensure that the client gets value for money for the budgets.
- Monitor and measure the effectiveness of all campaigns to ensure that the integrated approach is working.

An account director may have a team of account executives or account managers responsible for day-to-day project management. Depending on the size and structure of the agency, the account director may brief specialists directly or use an account team to handle the detail. Whatever the structure, it is vital that the account director sets and controls the overall integrated marketing strategy.

Planning Director

The planning director is a vital contributor to overall strategy and ensures that the integrated solution takes advantage of the individual marketing activities. The planning director in a traditional agency tends to come from a research or media background and will be responsible for selecting the media on a press, television or radio campaign.

While this remains an important part of the process on an integrated marketing campaign, planning has a much broader role - to select the most appropriate media and marketing techniques to achieve the client's overall objectives. The planner must have the depth of understanding to evaluate the strengths and contribution of direct marketing, sales training, sales promotion or retail development and the ability to balance these elements to achieve effective results. Planning is more of a marketing function than a media function in an integrated marketing agency. The planning director has a significant input to the development of the client's brief and will be in close contact with the client during the initial development stages of a campaign. As the campaign or project is implemented, the planning director must monitor performance against objectives and continue to analyze the effectiveness of all media in the overall campaign.

Integrated marketing is a dynamic process and the solution must be flexible enough to adjust to changing market conditions. Tactical elements like niche marketing, sales promotion, incentives or direct marketing can be used to fine-tune a campaign while the long-term strategic campaign operates in the background. The planning director must keep a constant watch on the client market in order to be in a position to make those fine adjustments.

Creative director

The creative director is responsible for providing the creative integrity that is essential to integrated marketing. In a traditional agency the creative director produces creative solutions for specific press or TV campaigns, but in an integrated agency has a much wider role. The creative solutions must continue to be of the highest calibre – achieving real impact, meeting communications objectives and winning awards on occasion – but it is also important that they can be easily translated into other media.

A single creative solution has to work across television, press, direct mail, brochures, point-of-sale, posters, training packs, customer literature and many other media – and it not only has to work, it must reflect consistency and be cost effective. A creative director in an integrated agency needs to have broad above and below the line experience to be able to judge the effectiveness of work in all media and to understand the practical limitations of different media.

The creative director will establish overall creative strategy in line with the planning director and the client team. The detailed creative work in each of the media is handled by individual teams of writers and art directors or designers with experience of specific media. An agency might employ several creative teams to work on above the line programmes and use copywriters and graphic designers to handle below the line projects which are primarily print-based. All of their work, however, is controlled by the creative director.

It is not just the creative effectiveness of the solutions that is important – the results must be cost effective and of high quality. Visual standards, for example, are critical in integrated marketing – the consistent use of corporate typefaces, illustration style, layout, colours, materials and other design criteria is a key element in presenting a consistent visual image across every campaign element. So an important part of the creative director's role is evaluating the use of specialists and external suppliers to ensure that work meets required standards.

Agency team

The account director, planning director and creative director are the core team in an integrated agency, but there are many other people who contribute to the success of a campaign. Some of them have already been mentioned:

- Account teams who handle the day-to-day programmes with agency specialists. The teams might include an account manager/executive, planners and creative team. Although the teams may work on different accounts or specialize in different areas of activity, it is vital that they work as teams so that their work is coordinated.
- An agency might include functional specialists such as direct marketing, incentives, training and training executives but they would only be employed on a permanent basis if there was sufficient volume of work to justify their presence. If the agency is using and coordinating external specialists, it would use project managers or buyers to coordinate their activities.

Media planning

Media planning and buying is a critical part of agency management. Depending on agency turnover and size this can be handled inside the agency or by an external specialist. A large agency with a high media spend might buy its own media, negotiating discounts with the media owners and obtaining the best position and deals for the client. However, there is a continuing debate in the business about role and value of media independents.

Media independents only buy media but, by bringing together purchases from a large number of different clients, they are able to increase their buying power and negotiate better overall deals. Media independents would also claim to offer greater levels of expertise in planning and buying because they can afford to recruit and retain the best people to concentrate on that activity. It makes sense for an integrated marketing agency to use media independents. Television, press and radio only represent a part of an integrated marketing strategy and it is logical that the planning group should be free to make unbiased recommendations.

However, it is also essential that an integrated marketing agency buys media effectively and it is therefore able to take advantage of the media independents' greater clout. This is a two-stage process. First the integrated marketing agency centralizes all media expenditure from a number of different product groups or operating divisions. This in itself can save the client money directly and indirectly through reduced administration. By utilizing experienced media specialists, the agency can then make a second level of savings.

Ideal structure

There is probably no ideal structure for an integrated marketing agency. Although the examples have described a single agency where a key coordinating group head up a team of specialists, there are a number of possible variations:.

Integrated marketing consultancy

An integrated marketing consultancy with a small core team of planning director, account director and creative director who work with external suppliers such as creative consultants, media independents and design consultancies. The consultancy carries out a coordinating function but it may lack the overall project management skills and quality control that is available in an integrated marketing agency.

Agency and consultancy

An above the line and below the line agency working in partnership. The above the line agency sets the overall strategy and works with a key account group within the below the line agency. Creative strategy is integrated and the two agencies can utilize each other's strengths to develop the most effective campaigns.

This kind of arrangement is ideal where a client has established relations with a major agency which offers a good above the line service but does not have the resources to offer additional below the line services. It is also valuable for the below the line agency which can offer an integrated service below the line but does not have the experience to offer above the line recommendations. The key to success in this kind of partnership is for the two organizations to create a joint strategic team which develops the overall strategy in conjunction with the client and maintains regular review meetings to ensure that the strategy is being implemented effectively.

Group of companies

A group with independent companies offering specialist services would, in theory, offer an integrated service but there may be internal barriers to achieving this which were described earlier in the chapter. While the group may have all the resources to provide an integrated service, it is essential for the client to have a central point of contact so that all services can be integrated.

Of these alternative solutions, the most successful is likely to be the integrated marketing consultancy because it offers no barriers and is committed to integration, but practical considerations and politics may force a working compromise.

Integrated marketing agency skills

Because integrated marketing embraces so many different disciplines, a full service integrated marketing agency will need to employ many different skills. The core skills of creative direction, account management and planning have already been described and the book makes the point that these jobs are different from those in conventional agencies because they require the vital element of coordination.

Integrated marketing agencies also need to employ specialists in all of the integrated marketing disciplines including direct marketing, public relations, advertising, retail and distributor relations, sales promotion, telemarketing, training, incentive programmes.

While the staff may not actually handle all these tasks themselves – they may manage the services of external specialists – it is vital that each discipline is represented within the agency. To add to the basic creative skills, integrated marketing staff need to develop other complementary skills:

- An ability to understand the contribution of other media and to integrate different elements to improve overall success.
- Programme management skills to coordinate and manage large complex projects with many different elements to improve overall success.
- Programme management skills to coordinate and manage large projects with many different elements.
- Administration skills to ensure that the different elements are brought together in a cost-effective way. These skills can be developed through training, but they may need to be imported though recruitment from outside the industry.
- Marketing and planning skills, for example, go beyond the normal agency planning disciplines so that a background in general marketing may be more important.
- Project management skills and administrative skills can be developed in any industry and may be more suitable with general management or marketing experience on the client side where the budget responsibilities are much broader.
- Creative skills developed within a single discipline need to be broadened to provide an appreciation and understanding of contribution and relationship of other media.

An agency that claims to offer a full-service integrated marketing solution must demonstrate a broad range of skills and operate a skills development programme that enables staff to improve their skills and offer clients increasingly higher standards of service.

Selecting an agency

While it is easy to adopt the term integrated marketing, few agencies are in a position to offer a full service. In selecting an agency, there are a number of key factors to assess:

- Commitment to integrated marketing – what is the agency's philosophy and how does it work in practical terms?
- Track record – what campaigns has the agency produced and how effective have their results been?
- Reputation – does the agency have a record for integrated marketing among the people that really matter – the clients?
- Accountability – how does the agency measure the performance of their campaigns and how does it hold itself accountable for success and client profitability?

- Client relationships – what is the agency's current client list and what percentage of these clients are enjoying long-term relationships. What is the average length of account tenure?
- Disciplines – does the agency offer all disciplines from within its own resources and can it offer the full range of services?
- Media balance – is the agency's structure balanced or is it biased towards any particular medium? An agency with a key dependence on above the line media may not be in a position to offer a truly independent assessment of the client's marketing needs.
- Staff – does the agency have the staff to handle complex integrated programmes? – What is the agency's recruitment and personal development policy?
- Creative reputation – does the agency and its staff have a reputation for outstanding creative work? What awards has it won? Are these standards applied consistently across all media?
- Marketing skills – Does the agency have staff with marketing backgrounds who have an appreciation of the brand marketing process?
- Administrative skills – does the agency have an administrative infrastructure which can cope with the high levels of transactions on an integrated marketing account.
- Financial stability – what is the agency's recent performance? Does it have the stability and resources to sustain an effective level of service over the long term?
- Structure – is the agency structured in a way that facilitates integrated marketing? Is the agency structured as a series of independent profit centres which are effectively competing for business? What is the level of coordination within the agency?
- Account management – does the agency offer a single point of contact for all campaigns and projects?
- What is the operating structure for detailed work within the agency?
- What is the agency's relationship with external suppliers?
- How does the agency control supplier standards? Does it utilize qualitative processes to manage suppliers?

This checklist can be a valuable means of assessing candidate agencies for an integrated marketing account and for monitoring the performance of the existing supplier. A relationship with an integrated marketing agency is a long-term relationship and it is important that the agency develops its service to meet the clients' changing needs.

Client/agency relationships

Contact and an effective working relationship is integral to the successful implementation of an integrated marketing programme. The ideal relationship is an agency contact working with one client contact so that every element of a campaign is coordinated and produced from a central source. Clients have commented on the simplicity of the relationship. It means that they do not have to go through a new learning process each time a new project is briefed. This reduces the time spent on briefing and can improve the overall effectiveness of marketing programmes. Meetings are an integral part of any agency/client relationship and they fall into three main categories:

- Strategic meetings
- Review meetings
- Project meetings.

Strategic meetings

These are held, say, annually or quarterly. The agency team of planning director, account director and creative director meet the key client contacts to discuss the overall marketing strategy and to prepare a marketing and communications strategy for the forthcoming period.

Review meetings

These are held quarterly, monthly or annually, with the same key contacts meeting to review progress and performance on specific campaigns and to provide an update on any important issues or marketing developments that might impact on the account. This type of meeting is essential if the agency claims to be accountable for the quality of its work and it also provides an opportunity to take any action to deal with short-term tactical requirements.

Project meetings

These are held regularly to put specific campaigns or projects into action. The agency and client formulate the brief and, at subsequent meetings, present and review proposals and progress on each activity.

Given the complexity of an integrated marketing campaign, it makes sense for both agency and client to use formal procedures for project management.

Marketing plan

Copies of the marketing plan and the overall strategy should be circulated to key members of the team on both client and agency side.

Visual standards

Maintaining visual standards is essential to the consistency of all integrated marketing programmes. Corporate guidelines should be issued to everyone responsible for communications material.

Briefing procedures

A standard format for project briefing should be developed and copies circulated to each member of the project team with action notes to cover essential activities.

This form of documentation is standard practice in both above and below the line agencies, but it is particularly valuable in the complexity of an integrated marketing account.

Agency/supplier relationships

Control and quality are essential here. The integrated marketing agency promises creative integrity, consistent standards and adherence to budget. If it is using external suppliers there, the suppliers need to work to the same standards and their performance should also be measurable. Many agencies are treating their key suppliers as business partners and developing long-term relationships with them, as well as developing joint quality standards that ensure overall consistency of performance. The supplier gets security work and the agency dependable, reliable performance. BS 5750 registration is increasingly used to maintain standards and to establish operating standards in the way in which suppliers:

- Respond to a brief or an enquiry
- Manage their own internal processes
- Check the accuracy and quality of their work
- Account for the time and cost of the work
- Meet delivery deadlines.

As well as imposing quality standards on their suppliers, integrated marketing agencies also need to develop effective working relationships that help the supplier to achieve effective results:

- Provide the supplier with copies of the overall marketing strategy.
- Review the marketing and creative strategy and explain the supplier's role in the process.
- Demonstrate the relationship between the supplier's work and other elements of an integrated marketing programme.

- Provide the supplier with practical support and information such as corporate guidelines or visual standards manuals.
- Give the supplier a comprehensive brief and provide a contact point for further information.
- Provide the supplier with feedback on the performance of the activity and the overall campaign.
- Wherever possible work with the supplier on joint projects to improve overall service performance.

These actions not only ensure a consistently high standard of performance but also help to build strong relationships between agency and supplier – and that is essential to improved overall solutions.

Summary

An integrated marketing agency can take a number of forms, although the ideal situation is one where a single agency handles all marketing activities through a single point of contact. Some clients have tried hybrid solutions, working with main agency and a consultancy to coordinate all below the line activities. The key team within an integrated marketing agency is the account director, responsible for all contact with the client, the planning director, responsible for integrating all the elements of the campaign, and the creative director, responsible for ensuring consistent creative standards across all work. The agency is also responsible for managing relationships with specialist external suppliers to ensure that every element of an integrated campaign is produced to the same high standards.

9 Managing the process

Introduction

Managing integrated marketing involves risk. A marketing director who has built up relations with proven suppliers over a period of years, who knows the difference between above and below the line, and who knows the need to respect specialists is asked to put everything into one agency and to manage the entire process of client/agency relationship through a single point of contact. The change can bring all the marketing and communications benefits of integrated marketing, but it requires a significant investment in the way that the marketing and communications functions are managed:

- Rationalization of the specialist functions
- A single point of contact for all agency/client relationships
- Appointment of a single agency or consultancy
- Reduction in headcount
- Changing responsibilities for key marketing and communications staff.

The single most important change to emerge is that one person emerges as the prime contact between agency and client and that person has total responsibility for coordinating all marketing communications activities, briefing and liaising with the agency and ensuring that the client specialists are able to channel their experience, skills and knowledge into briefing the agency and making the most of each project. Although this change appears to diminish the role of the specialist, in many cases it can free them for more profitable marketing activities and enable them to concentrate on providing the highest levels of customer service.

Traditional structures

Integrated marketing can change the traditional client/marketing and communications structure completely, so it is worth looking at a number of examples in detail.

Consumer products

The marketing director has overall responsibility for marketing strategy and implements programmes through a group of brand managers who in turn use the resources of a central marketing services group. Any marketing programme utilizes at least three members of the team: the marketing director, the brand manager, and the marketing services specialist. Within the marketing services group there are specialists covering advertising, public relations, sales promotion, retail development, direct marketing, packaging and incentive programmes. The sales director is also responsible for providing sales support for individual brand development programmes. Below the marketing services team are a range of specialist suppliers – advertising agency, public relations consultancy, sales promotion house, direct marketing agency, incentive marketing agency, design consultancy, printers and telemarketing consultants.

If each of the brand groups carried out its own programmes, there could be a proliferation of messages, visual styles and creative approaches with a considerable overlap in communications activities. There is also a heavy use of executive and administrative time in developing a brief, setting a creative strategy, selecting the agency and briefing the agency and other specialists. The administrative burden related to each job is also high: vetting the supplier, issuing purchase orders, handling multiple invoices, settling accounts and monitoring agency performance. The consequence is proliferation, and although the results can be effective in raising brand share they may be achieved at a cost.

Business-to-business products

If we look at the business-to-business sector a similar pattern emerges, although the role of the brand managers is less clearly defined. There may be a single marketing manager for a range of different products with perhaps separate marketing managers for each division in a large group. The central marketing services group may be replaced by group or divisional publicity managers with specialist staff such as design managers, public relations managers, exhibition specialists, direct mail managers or editorial managers. In addition to those, there may be a group public relations function to handle corporate and financial relations. In the business-to-business sector it is not just the marketing managers who would be involved in the briefing – product managers and technical managers would also be involved because of the complexity of the product. With more focus on below the line activities in this sector, the opportunities for proliferation are much greater.

Services marketing

The professional services sector may well be closer to an ideal model for integrated marketing for the simple reason that they are later into marketing. Legislation during the 1980s allowed many professionals to advertise for the first time, while a growth in the scale of practices meant that marketing has only recently become important. In smaller practices, responsibility for marketing may rest with a senior partner or a marketing specialist appointed from outside. A growing number of practices are appointing small groups of specialists to handle activities such as publications, but the high profile practice advertising would be channelled through a single source.

Limitations of the single structure

The traditional structure has worked well, but it has its limitations. Each of the marketing services and product specialists and each of the product/brand managers is looking to achieve the best results for their own particular territory and each is looking to win the major share of the budget and take the credit for any spectacular campaign successes. That does not create the right environment for a successful integrated campaign. Budgets must inevitably be allocated on the basis of individual departmental needs rather than overall strategy and the largest slice of the budget will go to those in the most powerful bargaining position or with the highest profile campaigns.

Single point of contact

The key to success in integrated marketing is to provide a single point of contact for all communications activities. As Sally Line marketing director Linda McCleod pointed out, 'I have a single point of contact for all my communications activities from television campaigns to brochures'. This means that the agency and all its specialists are being briefed by a single person. The brief will be consistent and each creative solution will be evaluated from the same point of view.

The choice of that single point of contact is perhaps the most difficult part of the process because it needs to be someone whose judgement is respected by the brand managers, product managers and other specialists who have traditionally looked after their own interests. The marketing director or the group publicity manager is likely to be the key contact, although on a major account there may be a small team of marketing specialists. The appointment of a single point of contact is dependent on the successful appointment of a single agency with the skills and resources to handle every aspect of the programme. The key skills for the single point of contact should be:

- Understanding of the contribution of each element of an integrated marketing programme
- Experience to evaluate the quality of integrated solutions
- The stature to deal with senior specialists on the client side
- Project management skills to coordinate complex programmes of overlapping activities
- Ability to integrate conflicting requirements into a coordinated brief that achieves overall marketing objectives and tactical objectives for different product groups and market sectors
- Budget control to coordinate and manage budgets from a number of different sources.

The successful coordinator is likely to have a balanced portfolio of marketing experience, project management skills and the sense of a career diplomat in order to try to meet the requirements of hungry product managers. It helps that integrated marketing can be measured because the agency can then be made accountable for its creative work and its marketing recommendations. One of the most powerful arguments for integrated marketing and one that can be used to quell opposition is that each element of the mix can be evaluated in relation to the overall success of the campaign.

Reducing headcount

This is perhaps the most controversial aspect of integrated marketing – it enables a company to reduce its headcount and this contributes indirectly to an overall cost saving. If we look at the work involved in the launch of a new product such as a car, it is easy to see how the workload grows – this is not job creation, it is simply a fact of life that every aspect of the programme has to be managed effectively.

Launch advertisements

Develop a brief for the agency
Evaluate media and creative proposals
Monitor insertions
Purchase orders for media
Check insertions against billings
Handle enquiries from direct response advertisements
Fulfil requests for information from direct response advertisements.

Launch public relations

Develop a public relations brief
Develop proposals with a consultancy
Organize press conferences and interviews
Provide press packs for launch events
Deal with press enquiries
Develop feature articles.

Launch events

Select and book launch venue
Prepare audio visual and other presentation material
Prepare delegate launch packs
Invite delegates
Organize creative treatment for event
Coordinate product delivery
Select and brief special event suppliers
Handle purchase orders and administration of special event suppliers.

Salesforce and dealer communications

Develop briefing pack for salesforce
Coordinate design, copy and print for briefing packs
Administration and selection of design and print suppliers
Coordination with training agency to produce product training material
Production and administration of training material
Development of sales incentive programmes using incentive specialists
Administration of incentive programme.

Customer direct marketing

Development and utilization of customer database
Brief direct marketing agency on creative marketing strategy
Administration for direct marketing campaign
Brief design, copy and production of consumer literature
Fulfilment of customer literature requests
Appointment and coordination of telemarketing agency
Integration of local marketing follow-up with central direct marketing programme.

Point-of-sale

Develop brief for display and point-of-sale campaign;
Brief suppliers and administration of design, production and distribution of point-of-sale material.

The above is an oversimplified version of the administrative and management processes in a major product launch. In reality the processes are much more complex with more and more meetings, as specifications and market conditions change. If we multiply this single product and campaign by the number of projects going through an organization in a year it is easy to see why the process is so time consuming. With integrated marketing the agency is responsible for coordination and administration of all specialist suppliers. The client develops the brief and receives a single invoice for all activities.

The management of integrated marketing has parallels in other areas of business. With the continued drive to reduce costs and concentrate on core activities, more companies are outsourcing services that can be handled efficiently by an independent specialist. The outsourcing service need not simply cover the tasks themselves, it can also include the management and coordination of different suppliers to provide the client with an integrated service. In the IT sector for example, managed service and facilities management are two different ways of handling IT service outside the company.

In facilities management, the service supplier provides complete service on the client's IT installation, in many cases taking over the running of the equipment. They charge the client for the service contract. In managed service, the service company may not handle all the service itself, particularly if the equipment comes from a number of different sources. The managed service contractor coordinates all the activities of the other suppliers, ensuring that they deliver on time, within budget to the required standard. They then coordinate the administration and invoicing and present the client with a single line invoice.

The client benefits from a consistent standard of service and simplified administration. It also helps the client to make better use of support staff who would previously have been tied down in day-to-day administration or delivery of service. They can now be used to handle strategic development tasks and other functions which are now possible. Some companies may take the opportunity to reduce headcount but this demonstrates that outsourcing can be used to improve the utilization of internal resources. By applying the same principles to marketing staff, it should be possible to divert specialist staff to functions that are more important to the company's long-term success – for example, relationship marketing or one-to-one marketing.

Introducing integrated marketing

This section is based on a proposal used within a life assurance company to implement an integrated marketing approach. The company took a cautious approach working with its existing advertising agency and appointing a below the line specialist to coordinate the below the line activities in partnership with the main agency.

The text is based on an internal report to the management team.

Key objectives

To succeed in the protection market, the company has identified a number of key success factors:

- Expand the market through product/customer segmentation
- Align sales channels more closely to product/customer segmentation
- Concentrate on brand development, rather than individual product communication
- Improve customer and sales understanding of the company's 'Service' approach and relate it to the concept of customized products
- Strengthen customer relationships
- Improve the targeting of different customer groups.

Setting an overall integration strategy

Integrated marketing will enable the company to achieve those objectives. In its simplest form, the integrated marketing programme would operate at two levels:

- Concentrate above the line activities on branding activities that reinforce the 'service for life' concept. Targeted communications can then be used to reinforce that concept and succeed in individual market sectors.
- Rationalize and integrate below the line activities to ensure that the brand proposition is reinforced and exploited in every communication with customers and sales channels.

In practical terms, this will require close working cooperation between the advertising agency and the below the line consultancy to ensure that creative themes are harmonized and sector activity is effective.

Make use of your database

Segmentation is a critical part of the overall process and it is vital that you develop an effective database to improve:

- Levels of information available to the sales channels and communications specialists
- The accuracy of targeted sector activity.

The database that is currently resident in the customer service unit will form a good basis. The information in the database should be easily accessible to marketing and sales specialists and there should be an ongoing programme of database enhancement:

- Capturing data from direct marketing or direct response activities
- Integrating information from planned customer and product audits and other forms of research
- Using profiling techniques and external sources to introduce new prospects into the database.

The current database information on existing customers can be utilized immediately to provide sales leads and opportunities for the first stage in a targeted mailing programme.

Ensure consistent visual and copy standards

Targeted communications are an integral part of the programme, but it is vital that every communication reflects and reinforces the overall identity and branding:

- Continue the literature redesign programme and ensure that agreed visual standards are applied to all forms of communication.
- Develop copy standards and key positioning messages that are included in every communication.
- Monitor visual and copy standards centrally.

Improve sales channel awareness and understanding

The new service-led approach is likely to require changes in the way the sales channels operate and communicate with customers. An integrated programme must include communications that ensure awareness and understanding of the new approach:

- Introductory communications explaining the benefits of the service-led approach
- Information on the availability and use of the database with examples of targeted approaches
- Training material that demonstrates how products can be customized to market sectors
- Regular product information that is related to the overall strategy
- Information on the other communications activities that support the direct sales activities, i.e. current advertising and direct marketing campaigns.

Operate a programme of targeted mailings

The database can be used to develop a programme of targeted mailings that build long-term customer relationships, rather than offer ad hoc product information:

- Introductory mailings to existing customers explaining the changing role of the salesforce – consultants who can tailor the company's services to meet their changing needs for life
- Targeted mailings that follow up the consultancy phase and offer the customer specific proposals
- Regular updates on new products or services that match the customer profile
- Targeted mailings to new prospects that introduce the service-led approach and build relationships.

Integrate other communications activities

Advertising and direct marketing will be the critical activities in building a successful customer/product segmentation programme. In the longer term, other marketing activities should be fully integrated to reinforce the core activities:

- Telemarketing
- Customer relationship activities and sales incentives
- Sponsorship activities
- Events.

Benefits of the integrated approach

An integrated approach, with the advertising agency and below the line consultancy working together, will ensure that you achieve your key objectives:

- Strengthen the core branding of a service-led company
- Effectively penetrate target markets
- Improve sales channel support and performance
- Build stronger customer relationships.

Summary

Introducing integrated marketing involves a high level of risk. It means replacing product and marketing specialists with responsibility for specific activities with one point of contact and, possibly, a single agency. The contact must therefore have the skills and experience to carry out the crucial role of the contact. Implementing a single point of contact can reduce the burden on other staff and simplify the process of coordination and administration.

10 Going integrated

Introduction

If, after reading this book, you want to go down the integration route, this chapter will give you a brief reminder of the key facts about integrated marketing. Use it as a checklist to develop your own strategy for direct marketing.

Why integrate?

Which of the following benefits would be important to your business?

- Creative integrity
- Consistency of messages
- Unbiased marketing recommendations
- Better use of all media
- Greater marketing precision
- Operational efficiency
- Cost savings
- High calibre consistent service
- Easier working relations
- Greater agency accountability.

How many different media do you use and are the messages presented consistently in each?

If you are marketing business products, how complex is the decision-making structure?

Have you researched how your customers perceive you. Do these perceptions match the messages in different publications?

Do you include consistent messages in all your publications?

Do you deal with specialist suppliers or a single agency? Do you feel you are getting unbiased advice on communications strategy?

Do you utilize different media to support each other? How well integrated are your current campaigns?

How precise is your marketing? Do you rely on advertising and other techniques which can only reach a limited audience?

How do you deal with your agency or agencies? Can you see advantages in simplifying the relationship?

Can you identify areas where integrated marketing would help you to reduce costs?

How accountable is your agency and how could you measure their performance?

Can you identify an opportunity to introduce an integrated marketing pilot project?

Building blocks

How do you currently use the building blocks of an integrated marketing campaign?

Can you see opportunities to improve the effectiveness of your communications by integrating other activities?

How do you use advertising?

Are you using direct marketing to support other marketing activities?

Could you use telemarketing to improve follow-up or lead generation?

Does your press information programme relate to your other marketing activities?

How effective is your internal communications programme?

Could you use sales promotion and incentives to improve different aspects of your marketing operations?

How well do your salesforce and your distributors understand their role in an integrated marketing programme?

Is your product information integrated with the rest of your communications programme?

Does your corporate identity reflect your current marketing objectives and planned perceptions?

Are you using relationship marketing to strengthen customer loyalty?

Approaches to planning

What are your overall business objectives?

What are your key marketing objectives?

How could integrated marketing help you to achieve those objectives?

Have you researched internal and external perceptions of your company and your products?

How complex is the decision-making process for your product or service? Could integrated marketing help you reach all decision makers more effectively?

Can you identify the main concerns of your target audience?

What are your planned perceptions and are you communicating them consistently?

Can you establish integrated communications objectives?

What are the key media for achieving your communications objectives?

Scenarios for integrated marketing

Does your company face complex issues in the marketplace, or do your products raise complex issues within the customer company?

To market your products or services effectively, do you have to convince many different decision makers? Does your communications programme work consistently across all decision makers?

Are you involved in market development projects and is it essential that you carry out market education as well as developing sales?

Are you operating through multiple sales channels and is it essential that each one of these operates effectively?

Are you introducing new product programmes and do you need to convince different groups of people that your products will benefit that organization?

Does research show that important decision makers and influencers hold poor perceptions of your organization and, if so, is it vital that you reposition the organization?

Do you have a limited budget which means that every element of the programme must work harder? Do some media represent better value for money?

Are you operating in niche markets and do you need to ensure that your marketing performance is consistent across all sectors?

Is your company undergoing significant change and do you need to ensure that messages are communicated consistently to every member of the target audience?

Are you introducing a local marketing strategy and do you wish to ensure that you offer consistent levels of service and support throughout a network?

Supporting your business objectives

How could integrated marketing help you to improve your sales performance?

Is the quality of lead generation sufficiently high?

Could integrated support material improve the performance of the salesforce?

How could you use integrated marketing to improve relationships with customers?

Do you want to build partnership with your key accounts?

How could you use integrated marketing to introduce the concept of partnership?

Do your partnership communications reach all the decision makers?

Could you use techniques like seminars or executive briefings to improve partnership?

Is your organization focused on customers?

Who are the key targets for customer focus communications?

How important is customer focus to your organization?

Is your organization facing major change?

Which are the key audiences to communicate the impact of change?

How important is local marketing performance to your business?

What type of support do you give to your local outlets and how could integrated marketing improve performance?

How successful have your product launches been? Could integrated marketing improve performance?

Are you using the full range of communications techniques to launch products?

Is your company committed to quality?

How effectively do you communicate quality and how could this be improved?

Customer contact strategies

Have you audited internal and external perceptions of your business?

What do you need to do to change perceptions of your company?

What are the elements of your customer contact strategy?

How can integration improve the quality of your customer contact strategy?

Agency structure

Is your agency committed to integrated marketing? What is the agency's philosophy and how does it work in practical terms?

What integrated campaigns has the agency produced and how effective have their results been?

Does the agency have a record for integrated marketing amongst the people that really matter - the clients?

How does the agency measure the performance of its campaigns and how does it hold itself accountable for success and client profitability?

What is the agency's current client list and what percentage of these clients are enjoying long-term relationships? What is the average length of account tenure?

Does the agency offer all disciplines from within its own resources and can it offer the full range of services?

Is the agency's structure balanced or is it biased towards any particular medium?

Does the agency have the staff to handle complex integrated programmes – what is the agency's recruitment and personal development policy?

Does the agency and its staff have a reputation for outstanding creative work. What awards has it won? Are these standards applied consistently across all media?

Does the agency have staff with marketing backgrounds who have an appreciation of the brand marketing process?

Does the agency have an administrative infrastructure which can cope with the high levels of transactions on an integrated marketing account?

What is the agency's recent financial performance? Does it have the stability and resources to sustain an effective level of service over the long term?

Is the agency structured in a way that facilitates integrated marketing? Is the agency structured as a series of independent profit centres which are effectively competing for business? What is the level of coordination within the agency?

Does the agency offer a single point of contact for all campaigns and projects?

What is the operating structure for detailed work within the agency?

What is the agency's relationship with external suppliers?

How does the agency control supplier standards? Does it utilize qualitative processes to manage suppliers?

Managing the process

What is your current internal marketing structure?

Can you identify a person with the stature and experience to introduce and manage integrated marketing?

Are there opportunities to reduce headcount by introducing integrated marketing?

What would be your key objectives in introducing integrated marketing?

Can you identify key tasks in introducing integrated marketing?

How would you measure the success of the programme?

Index